A Chance to Dance

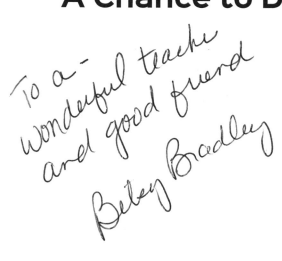

To a —
wonderful teacher
and good friend

Betsy Bradley

A Chance to Dance

—m—

A Parent's Guide to Healthy Dance Education

Betsy Bradley

ISBN: 1505366968
ISBN 13: 9781505366969

Dedication

To my sons, Ben and John,
who sat through many classes, rehearsals, and
performances so their mother could pursue something she
loves, thank you.

Foreword

by
Bruce and Colleen Hallberg

After watching several movies starring Fred Astaire, our eight-year-old son, David, came to us expressing a desire to tap dance. We looked at each other, wondering how parents support this interest and find dance lessons for an enthusiastic little boy.

We found a studio in Phoenix where David could learn tap and jazz, as those were the exciting styles he saw in the Fred Astaire movies. Several years later, after enrolling in Arizona School for the Arts, David was also introduced to ballet in the school's dance program. As parents, we were very supportive; however, we were not personally familiar with the dance world, and we were quite uneducated and inexperienced with parenting a budding young dancer.

A Chance to Dance is a wonderfully helpful book that we wish we had been able to reference when navigating the dance world as novice dance parents. This book covers many topics, from dancewear to ways of keeping your child grounded in their journey in dance to the trials of bullying that young male dancers can face.

We were told that our son had a natural talent for ballet, and we were very lucky to have Kee Juan Han to help us navigate proper instruction and direction for David. Not every parent has a trusted mentor as we did. There were still decisions only we as parents could make, and a reference like *A Chance to Dance* would have been a great support.

This book will be a helpful tool to all parents, whether their child is enjoying having dance as a part of life or choosing dance as a mainstay throughout his or her whole life. It will help guide you in a practical, easy-to-understand, no-nonsense manner, which, looking back, we would have found very useful.

—⚬—

The Hallbergs are the proud parents of two sons, Brian and David Hallberg. David, to whom they are referring here, is a principal dancer with American Ballet Theater and the first American dancer to hold the position of principal dancer with the famed Bolshoi Ballet.

Foreword

by
Kee Juan Han

As the current school director of the Washington School of Ballet and past director of Arizona School of Ballet who has taught worldwide, my goal has been to develop dancers as well as share the artistic heritage of ballet. I have had some wonderfully dedicated students—David Hallberg among them—who have gone on to solid careers in the dance world. I am equally proud of my students who have successfully pursued other careers with the help of the discipline and confidence they have found through studying dance.

During my twenty years of training dancers, I've seen so many parents who have misconceptions about the world of dance. There is a real need for good information and encouragement for parents who want to know how and when they should get involved with their child's dance education.

Betsy Bradley is a dance teacher, educator, and parent; her book is a good source of information and guide for dance parents.

Table of Contents

I

Choosing Dance

Dance has the triple distinction of being a physical discipline, an intellectual exercise, and an artistic endeavor. To train in dance, a student is called on not just to use his or her brain and body, but also to make a connection between the two in order to achieve fluidity and execute the choreography.

When this book talks about a dancer, it includes both boys and girls. All the benefits and positive experiences of dance are equally available to both genders. Although many people think of dance as being exclusively for girls, it only takes one trip to the ballet or musical theater to see the strength, agility, and poise both male and female performers possess.

—m—

Several children's books address the subject of boys who dance. My favorite is Max *by Rachel Isadora. It tells the story of a little brother who follows his sister to her ballet class.* Oliver Button

Is a Sissy, another good one by Tomi de Paola, shows the struggles Oliver encounters as he pursues his passion for tap dancing—that is, until his peers see him perform.

—‍⁓‍—

Although certain body types (which are addressed in chapter 6) are considered ideal for various styles of dance, all body types will benefit from the exercises that form the basis for ballet, modern/contemporary dance, and jazz. Dance encourages still bodies to stretch regularly and with purpose. It slowly induces inwardly rotated hips and pigeon-toed feet to turn out, bringing the body back to a straight line. Age-old class exercises straighten the back and strengthen the now-famous "core."

Dancing helps develop muscles in the legs and arms. Under proper supervision, these muscles become long and lean, as opposed to the short, bulky muscles of a weight lifter or football player. Dance students have the advantage over athletes because dance classes include exercises to increase flexibility, which reduces injury and muscle strain.

—‍⁓‍—

"Real men lift women," reads a quote from the T-shirt of a dancer with the Oklahoma City Ballet.

—‍⁓‍—

Concentration and focus are a large part of dance education. As part of class curriculum, students are required to follow instruction and control their bodies, their voices, and their expressions in an age-appropriate manner. The discipline, focus, and self-control developed through dance training transfer to other areas of the student's life is an added bonus.

—∞—

Time and time again, I have seen the pride that particularly wiggly children show as they master these skills and gain self-control, coordination, and strength.

—∞—

Moreover, the dance thought process is like no other. Dance students prepare for and learn through practice and participation in class and performances. The process begins with learning, executing, and mastering combinations of steps. Next comes musicality. Dancers take each step in exact accordance with the music and synchronize their movements with the other dancers in the piece. They learn combinations of steps, or choreography, and execute them with the skill each step demands. Then they add the emotion required to convey the message and feeling of the story or dance. This is what puts the beauty and art into dance.

Dance-related skills like learning choreography, controlling the movement of the body, and understanding and incorporating corrections are unlike skills taught anywhere else. Deep understanding of math and excellent reading skills do not prepare you for dance. Dance requires a brain aptitude that only the demands of dance can develop.

—⟋⟍—

Parents have told me they put their child in dance in order to help them focus. They specifically chose dance classes over drug therapy for an attention deficit. They wanted the child to learn a discipline that would "make the focusing muscle work." As a teacher, I can tell you it works for some children but does not succeed for all.

—⟋⟍—

—⟋⟍—

One mother explained how her child was progressing in dance class. This sweet little girl had a bit of an attention problem. She was distracted but never disruptive; the term spacey comes to mind. The mother mentioned that her child was starting to "get it" about fifty percent of the time. Even if the student's learning stalls there, she will be fifty percent better off than when she started. If

*she never gets to a hundred per-
cent, she will still be using a part of
her brain in a way she did not use
it before. She has learned how to
process information in a completely
different way than she would have if
she had never studied dance.*

—⁓—

The collaboration between students in dance classes and performances is another benefit to studying this art form. Dancers are trained to dance in unison and work together to perform the dance. Students learn spatial awareness by finding their space in class and on the stage. They share the confusion of learning the dance and the joy of accomplishing a finished product. That, and the thrill of the performance experience, allows close friendships to form and endure.

There is something special about performing on stage. The costumes, stage lights, makeup, and dressing rooms with lighted mirrors can make a student feel like a professional. Add to that beautiful music as accompaniment, and the thrill is palpable. A competent dance school will spend many months preparing students to step onto the stage. Rehearsals on the performance stage, along with supportive teachers and volunteers, help stage fright subside.

Meanwhile, on the other side of the curtain, families wait for the house lights to dim. Many have brought flowers for their rising stars. As the performance begins, there is no doubt it will be memorable, no matter what.

Starting Classes

Before beginning a dance class, students should first seek approval from a doctor. If a doctor has been seeing your child for well visits or for medical concerns such as asthma, scoliosis, or other health conditions, a conversation with that doctor is advised.

In most cases dance will not aggravate these conditions; it often can be beneficial to a student's health. Your doctor may suggest an added precaution if a condition is severe.

—∞—

I am aware of three dancers who overcame debilitating scoliosis during their dance training to become principal dancers in ballet companies. Others have successfully danced with asthma and diabetes.

—∞—

In countries that have government-run ballet schools, students begin training at eight years old. These students, chosen from auditions held throughout the country, are sent to a boarding school for their academic and ballet training. Often, a job at a government-subsidized company is waiting for them at the end of their studies.

In the United States, most families would not be interested in sending an eight-year-old away to train even if there were schools that offered this type of supervised program.

There are also no guaranteed jobs waiting at the end of a student's dance education, regardless of the chosen training path.

In countries where children routinely live with their parents through adolescence, children may begin in a pre-ballet program as early as four years old. The child should be able to separate from the parent and take part in a forty-five-minute to one-hour class of age-appropriate exercises.

Parents can find jazz classes for students as young as five or six years old. Each family must gain knowledge of the class curriculum, music, performance standards, and costumes to determine if they feel a class is appropriate for their young child. Different studios have different philosophies about the content of the class. Young students can start in combination classes that are specially designed for ages three or four.

Creative dance classes for early childhood years can also be found in certain communities.

Older Students

Students, especially boys, can begin dance training at later ages and successfully pursue a dance career. With girls, ten years old is usually the latest a beginner can start and still successfully train her body. There are exceptions, of course. There are those with physical gifts that allow them to achieve the required skills at a later age. Boys can often begin later and achieve success. Their strength surges around puberty, and their muscles seem to develop magically. However, they are still required to achieve flexibility, which is generally more difficult to attain with age.

Boys in beginning ballet class
Photo courtesy of Bender Performing Arts, Phoenix, Arizona

Pointe class, or beginning pointe, is incorporated into ballet class, and under no circumstances should it begin before age ten. It is not unusual for a school to start students as late as twelve years old. To accommodate the intricacies of pointe work, a student must have mastered a good deal of strength and correct body placement. Not all students achieve this level of competence. Either physical limitations or lack of adequate training can prevent a student from successfully tackling dancing in pointe shoes. There are students on the Internet who perform beautifully on pointe at a young age, but this is a rare exception to the rule and can causes physical problems later on.

Students who want to take ballet to augment their gymnastics or ice skating, or just to enjoy the movement, can start at any age. It is sometimes harder to find beginner classes for students ages twelve to sixteen. After sixteen years of age, they may be able to join beginner adult classes.

Adult Students

Many studios offer beginning to advanced dance classes in a variety of disciplines for adult students. They provide a fun and healthful way to either come back to what was once a childhood pursuit or to fulfill a dream you may have had as a child. It is never too late to dance.

—⚹—

An adult explains why she takes ballet classes: "I enjoy the piano music. My mom is an accomplished pianist, so piano music feels like home to me, and it's a workout that doesn't bore me."

—⚹—

Basic Costs

The costs of dance programs and equipment vary across the United States and throughout the world, but the requirements are the same: dancewear, shoes and tuition. Basic lessons require only the first three categories, so a student on a budget may participate without obtaining the extras that can add to the cost.

Tuition: cost of classes
Dancewear: leotards, tights, skirts, dance pants and tops, dance belt for boys
Shoes: ballet slippers, jazz shoes, tap shoes, pointe shoes

With dancewear and shoes, not every student will need everything listed. The students' needs will depend on the type of dance they pursue.

Other fees that frequently arise as your child becomes more involved in dance include the following:

Production fees: When a child participates in a school performance, the school often charges a production fee that helps offset the enormous cost of renting a theater and employing stagehands. Occasionally this fee is replaced with a requirement to purchase or sell a number of tickets.

Costume fees: This is occasionally included in the production fee when the costumes belong to the studio and not to the students. Some studios ask students to purchase each costume they will perform in. The cost can run from twenty-five dollars to hundreds of dollars, depending on the costume and the number of dances in which the student will perform.

Company fees: Studios may charge an annual fee for students accepted into a studio company.

Coaching fees: If a child chooses to participate in solo competitions, a coach usually works with that child to set choreography and rehearse on a one-on-one

basis. The choreographic fee and
the coaching fees may be charged
separately.

Competitions: Travel, lodging, and registration
fees are the responsibility of the
students and their families. Many
of these competitions award small
cash prizes or scholarships.

Costs are discussed in more detail in chapter 5.

Time Commitment

The time commitment your child makes to dance will
depend on a variety of factors. You will need to consider
the long-term goal for dancing, the child's enjoyment of the
classes, family and school commitments, and money.

Young dancers often start with one class a week, increas-
ing after the first or second year to two classes a week. Around
the age of eight or nine, a student committed to improve-
ment needs to take at least three classes a week. These classes
sometimes include different dance disciplines, as discussed
later in the book. It is not unusual for a committed middle
or high-school student to spend five or six days at the studio
each week, including classes and rehearsals.

Even spending so much time at the studio, most dancers do not allow their schoolwork to suffer. If they are good
students, they will continue to be so. If they are average or
struggling, with their dancing as an incentive, they sometimes
gain more focus. The discipline that dancers learn in class
often spills over and aids them in time management of their

responsibilities. (It won't necessarily help with cleaning their rooms, but it may help them with getting their schoolwork done in a timely manner.) Dedicated dance students take every available opportunity to keep up with schoolwork, often using study hall, time in school classes, and time traveling from home to the studio to complete assignments. If their dance classes are not back-to-back, they have time between classes to sneak in some homework. Long-term projects can be relegated to days with no dance classes or rehearsals. Sometimes this is only on Sundays.

Spending this much time together also encourages deep and lasting friendships. Sleepovers concluding with the whole group being dropped off at the dance studio are common.

—◊◊◊—

Many of the most dedicated dancers are in the top percentages of their classes in school. When I dedicated myself to dance, all my grades improved. That was with ten hours of classes and eight hours of rehearsals weekly. I have watched students move from dance to studying administration, science, and medicine at noted universities.

—◊◊◊—

II

Dance Styles

—❦—

The information in this chapter
will provide an overview of the
most popular types of dance training available in the United States.
Dance training for the physical and
emotional enjoyment of the art form
may be started at any age. The ages
suggested in this chapter are guidelines for students who are interested
in dance as a career.

—❦—

There are many types of dance instruction. The challenge is
finding the dance style that is best for your child and deciding
when he or she should begin training. The answers to these
and other questions depend on what you and your child want
out of their dance education. Some parents feel the decision
to enroll their child in dance lessons is their choice and theirs

alone, yet the success of the student depends as much on this or her own dedication to the classes as on natural ability.

—ɯ—

> I once taught a young girl dance who, though brimming with natural talent, did not continue classes beyond her first year. She was also a natural swimmer. When she would swim in a meet, she would receive a medal simply for participation. In addition, each time she won, she was awarded a trophy. For her, the regular gratification of medals outweighed the long wait for applause at an annual or semiannual dance recital. She lacked the joy of movement that would have motivated her to continue studying dance.

—ɯ—

Ballet

Ballet is a style of dance that stresses specific techniques that have been developed through the centuries and are infused with adaptations from different countries and different masters. It is recognizable by its precise movement, grace, classical steps, and poise. The first ballet school was founded in Paris, France, in the late 1600s. Ballet has become the basis for most forms of dance other than folk dancing.

—⁂—

In 2003, the book The Dancing Master *by P. Rameau was translated and republished from the original work, dated 1725. Among other things, the book outlines the positions of the feet still used today in ballet classes.*

—⁂—

Ballet provides the technical foundation that facilitates mastery of other dance forms. The strength, flexibility, balance, coordination, and musicality fundamental to ballet are also required in other forms of dance, including modern, lyrical, and jazz. Ballet, therefore, is a practical place for students to begin their training, regardless of the dance form they might later choose to pursue. Ballet class is also an appropriate

Photo by Michael Cook, courtesy of Tempe Dance, Tempe, Arizona

place for young children, as it complements their inno-
cence and wonder. Many studios offer classes for students
as young as four years old.

—⚭—

> The different techniques of ballet
> include Vaganova, from the Russian
> School; Cecchetti, from the Ital-
> ian School; and Bournonville, who
> was a choreographer and director
> whose specific style of ballet was
> taught at the Danish Ballet. The
> Royal Academy of Ballet (RAD) in
> England follows a specific syllabus
> that proceeds through graded lev-
> els and must be started at the first
> level. The Balanchine method is
> based on the unique movements of
> the great contemporary choreog-
> rapher George Balanchine. It is not
> unusual for a classical ballet studio
> in the United States to use a combi-
> nation of styles.

—⚭—

Character Dance

Character dance is stylized folk dance for ballet dancers.
It has been refined and adapted for performance, and it

plays a major role in many classical ballets. For instance, one can see it in the Spanish, Hungarian, and Neapolitan dances in *Swan Lake* or the mazurka and czardas in *Coppélia*. Character dance communicates the style, mood, or quality of movement and musical characteristics of its place of origin, but it is enhanced for the stage. Character dance classes are an important part of a ballet dancer's training; they help the student develop a deeper understanding of various styles of dancing. Girls wear skirts and shoes with heels, and boys wear either boots or shoes with low heels for class.

Photo by Lynn Battenberg, courtesy of Scottsdale
School of Ballet, Scottsdale, Arizona

Modern/Contemporary

Milton Myers Director of the Contemporary Program works
with students. Courtesy of Jacob's Pillow Dance Festival.
Photo by Kristi Pitsch

Modern dance places an emphasis on a dancer's own inter-
pretations instead of on structured steps. Modern dancers
favor movements derived from the expression of feelings.
Generally, modern techniques emphasize movement in the
torso, suppleness of the spine, and a more weighted quality
of movement. They often incorporate "fall and recovery"
series that take the dancer down to the floor and up again,
teaching the student to work with and against gravity.

During the 1900s, dancers began exploring and show-
casing this form of dance. The classical tutus were gone;
dances were often staged without scenery, and shoes were
abandoned in favor of bare feet. Silence, or a mere drum
beat, replaced the classical music that characteristically
accompanied ballet.

Modern dance, like character dance, is often offered as part of a complete ballet program for established students. Many times, contemporary ballet choreography includes modern dance techniques.

Modern dance studios in many metropolitan cities rival ballet studios. It is possible to study modern dance without ballet training. Nevertheless, just as modern dance training is essential to present-day ballet study, ballet training enhances a student's ultimate success in modern dance.

Some modern dance studios offer creative movement classes for very young students. This is another appropriate route for starting a young student's dance training.

—∿∿—

Like ballet, modern dance has a variety of techniques, which have blended together over time. Notable modern dancers include Merce Cunningham, Alvin Ailey, Paul Taylor, Alwin Nikolais, and Martha Graham, all are American modern dance pioneers whose styles are uniquely recognizable.

—∿∿—

Jazz

Jazz dance is inspired and developed by the rhythms and techniques of jazz music. As the music itself changes to represent popular culture, so too does jazz dance change. A handful of dancers/choreographers names shaped jazz dance, a uniquely American-born dance form.

Bill Hastings, Broadway veteran, works with Jazz/
Musical Theatre Dance Program participants.
Courtesy of Jacob's Pillow Dance Festival.
Photo by Kristi Pitsch

Jack Cole, Max Mattox, Luigi Faccuito, Gus Giordano, and Bob Fosse are a few of those who helped take jazz out of the clubs, into the dance studios, and onto the stage.

Jazz music is subtly infused with sexual tensions and innuendo, and so is the dance style it inspired. The movements often have a slinky or sensual quality. For this reason, jazz dance may not be an appropriate starting point for a young

A tap class
Photo by Lynn Battenberg, courtesy of Bender
Performing Arts, Phoenix, Arizona

dance student. Jazz dance, however, is a useful and important genre to study as an older dancer involved in ballet or modern dance. It teaches a relaxed and casual quality often used by choreographers from all backgrounds of dance. Along with ballet, classes in both jazz and tap are necessary for anyone who dreams of dancing on Broadway.

Lyrical jazz dance is not as impulse driven as jazz dance; it is more expressive, using the balletic sentiment but not classical ballet steps. It is usually offered in conjunction with jazz classes beyond beginner levels.

Tap

Tap is a form of dance distinguished by the use of metal taps attached to the toe and heel of the tap shoe. The dancer uses the shoes as percussive instruments, striking the floor to produce rhythms. These beats can be in sync with accompanying music, or they may involve a rhythm of the dancer's own making. Tap is unique in that it does not require a foundation in other dance forms although they can be helpful. Students can begin and enjoy tap dancing at any age. For students looking to dance on Broadway, in Las Vegas shows, or with the Rockettes, tap is a necessary skill to add to their ballet and jazz training.

Hip-Hop

Hip-hop is a relatively new form of dance to make its way into the dance studio. It originated on urban street corners. Hip-hop is often accompanied by rap music or beats. It involves a mix of pulsating bodies, gliding movements, and acrobatics. For those hoping to dance in music videos or some of the more contemporary Broadway shows, hip-hop is essential. Middle school, high school, and college students who like to be the life of the party also enjoy it.

Getting ready for a Hip-Hop class
Courtesy of Bender Performing Arts, Phoenix, Arizona

—ᘒ—

A professional hip-hop dancer, who began his professional career at fourteen years of age, pushes him-

self to take classes in many different styles. As quoted in the May/June 2015 issue of Dance Spirit *magazine, he advises, "Ballet, ballet, ballet—especially for boys! It's the foundation for everything."*

—⟋⟍—

Folk Dance

Irish, Flamenco, Russian, Indian, Chinese, and American Indian cultures each have defined styles of folk dance that can be studied in a classroom setting. Students of these dance styles can find performance opportunities in both competitive settings and professional companies. These classes may occasionally be found in general dance studios, but they also appear at cultural centers, community centers, and specialty schools.

—⟋⟍—

Once on stage, one of my students commanded all the attention; you could not take your eyes off her. Unfortunately, her flexibility and the structure of her feet did not allow her a true chance as a ballet performer. She worked with a Flamenco group, which allowed her to use her incredible stage presence while performing a style of dance that suited her and allowed for success.

—⧖—

Choosing a Dance Style

When you begin the search for the right dance class for your child, it is important that you consider your child's personality, the goals you want him or her to achieve while studying dance, and the level of commitment you and your child are willing to make.

If you want to calm a wild child, an age-appropriate ballet class may be a good place to start. If you want to encourage a young child's imagination, perhaps you should seek a creative dance class. Want to get rid of excess energy? Jazz or hip-hop may be a good fit. Tap is full of aerobic exertion but requires the same level of discipline and concentration as ballet.

Bear in mind, one can never predict whether or not a child will fall in love with dance and strive for a professional career. Beginning training with ballet will facilitate this possibility. When a child starts at seven or eight years old, ballet provides a solid basis for any other dance discipline the student may later choose to pursue.

—⧖—

A variety of classes are offered to students younger than eight years old. These classes prepare children for more serious study. They include pre-ballet, creative dance, parent and tot, and combo classes. Choosing the proper class for your child will be beneficial and fun as they wait for their body and mind to become prepared for more serious dance study. The ideal age to begin classical ballet training is eight years old. With the exception of hip-hop and tap, the other dance forms are more easily integrated once a dancer has established a solid ballet foundation.

—⟋⟍—

III

Choosing a Dance Studio

There are many things to look for to help your dance student succeed. The best dance training may or may not be available in the dance school closest to your home. An important point to remember when looking for a dance school is that a student who has been poorly trained will have to unlearn bad habits before he or she will be able to learn proper technique. At the start of your child's dance education, you will not know the level of his or her future commitment to dance. To avoid this pitfall, make sure the studio you choose has a keen understanding of technique and respect for the dance forms it offers.

Ballet Studios

A ballet school is a good place to start dance training regardless of the student's ultimate goal because ballet training supports a variety of other dance performance styles. If your child intends to perform with a ballet company, with a modern dance company, or in a Broadway or Las Vegas show, ballet will provide an excellent foundation.

If there is such a school in your community, a ballet school that is associated with a professional ballet company can provide a good place to start training. These schools usually focus on professional training. They often have strict rules about attendance, appropriate dress, and hair preparations. They will expect a student to take more classes as the level of achievement increases. They may also offer recreational programs as a separate option for the more casual student. As the student advances, the school will augment ballet technique classes with some, if not all, of the following: character, modern, Pilates, pointe, men's, partnering, or repertory classes, as well as rehearsals for upcoming performances.

A bonus to studying in a school associated with a professional dance company is that professional productions that need young students or fill-in corps work sometimes pull students from those classes. (The corps is the large group of dancers that performs within the ballet.) Students of exceptional ability may, upon graduation from the school, be offered a contract with the company.

The company brings in a school director, who works under the company's artistic director, the executive director, or the board of trustees. The school director compiles the syllabus, sets schedules, hires staff, teaches classes, oversees the school's performances, communicates with parents, and sets the tone of the school.

Observe and talk to the school director, if possible, when deciding whether or not to enroll your child in the school. Ask other parents who currently have or previously have had students in the school about their experiences with the school director. Often the director is a retired dancer who began teaching after retirement. For instance, the director may know the ballet technique needed for a successful performance career, but may not understand the needs of a family on a budget that is exploring activities that might interest their children. It will behoove you to ensure that your family can accommodate the school's expectations of you as a parent and your child as a student. For example, a student may not be allowed to change class levels to accommodate or simplify your family's schedule. Siblings may not be allowed to enroll or participate in the same classes unless they have similar levels of ability.

In some of the larger schools, the director has an assistant who acts as a liaison to the parents. While looking for a school, you can meet with this person instead of the director, as long as the assistant can answer all of your questions. If this person is unable to respond to your questions without checking with the director, then you may wish to ask to speak directly to the school director.

Teachers in these studios usually have extensive ballet training, as well as performance and teaching experience. Teachers lead classes relevant to their expertise. Although they may teach a variety of technique levels, they do not usually teach a variety of types of dance or related classes. A Pilates teacher should be trained and certified in that technique. Although a ballet teacher frequently teaches character dance, doing so also requires a great deal of specialized training. A female teacher usually teaches pointe class, and a male teaches the men's class.

The only way to teach ballet is through a series of instructions, corrections, feedback, and explanations of the steps. Teachers often need to put their hands on students to gently rotate a leg or adjust a head position. They accompany this physical adjustment with verbal instruction and allow students to "feel" the placement they have been unable to achieve on their own.

Most dance students will have an easier time in one aspect of dance than another. Some can turn or pirouette well; others jump high. Some are flexible, musical, or expressive in their gestures. There will always be something students can do better or a new skill they can learn that they have not yet mastered. Because of this, it is imperative that a student learn appropriate ways to work effectively. Positive reinforcement is not abundant in the ballet classroom, so students need to understand that teachers give corrections not out of spite or to embarrass the student but because they believe the child can accomplish and improve execution of the skills.

Dance schools vary greatly in corporate structure. Most ballet companies are nonprofit organizations with limited financial backing, and therefore, they have to watch every penny they spend. Through a bond fund or a wealthy patron, a school may have large studios that are clean and inviting. Within basic health parameters, any studio will do for a training facility, regardless of the grandeur or lack thereof. The floors of the studio are the most important physical element. (This is addressed later in this chapter.)

Studios should have dance barres mounted along the walls at two levels or portable barres that can be moved into place in the classroom. A well-equipped studio also has a wall of mirrors.

Private ballet studios differ greatly in quality, so it is important to know how to analyze the school for the best fit to your expectations. As previously stated, undoing bad training is difficult for both teacher and student. Even if you believe your child will not pursue ballet to an advanced level, it is best to give him or her quality training for several reasons. Your child may fall in love with ballet and choose to persevere; he or she could be injured unnecessarily through inappropriate teaching; and you deserve the best quality for the time and money you will invest in providing dance instruction to your child.

The studio owners are usually the directors of the school, and they often teach classes. You should know their background and expertise. A private ballet studio may be run by someone who simply enjoyed ballet as a child and has no professional or performance experience outside of annual recitals. Although the owner may be good hearted and sincere, your chances of getting solid training at this type of studio will not be as good as finding an owner with a larger variety of performance experiences. You may find an excellent teacher at this type of school, but the continuity of the program depends on a solid syllabus and consistent teaching at all levels.

Photo by Lynn Battenberg, courtesy of Scottsdale
School of Ballet, Scottsdale, Arizona

A private studio may also be owned and operated by a retired professional dancer with excellent teaching skills. Be aware that not all retired dancers make good teachers or understand the process required to develop a good dancer. They do, however, understand the dedication and hard work it takes to be a professional dancer, and they respect the art form. Again, you will want to observe classes and see if the style of teaching and the rapport between the teacher and the students is appropriate for your child. There a many excellent private studio's to be found.

Personalities and process can vary immensely from studio to studio. A director or teacher who was raised in an academy school in Poland will have a very different approach than one raised in a studio in America. Some may feel a strict Vaganova syllabus or Royal Academy of Dance program is the only way to run a school, others incorporate a combination of styles. Certain teachers express themselves loudly, others are unapproachable, and some are sensitive. Observe the classes and evaluate what works best for your child.

Jazz/Competition Studios (Including Tap and Hip-Hop)

Jazz instruction is frequently found in competition studios. A "competition studio" will often have one or more company levels that compete in the many competitions that tour the country annually. (Competitions are also addressed in chapter 8.) These studios will offer ballet to support the jazz and lyrical styles that are categories in the competitions. Other offerings at these studios may include tap, hip-hop, acrobatics, and, for the youngest students, combo classes.

You will want a competition studio if your child dreams of dancing in music videos, as a backup dancer for touring shows, on a cruise line, in Disney shows, or even on Broadway (although many of these performers are also ballet dancers). Dancers from these studios may also appear on television dance competitions. Competition studios are also beneficial to students interested in cheerleading and pom squads.

Competition studios are sometimes referred to as recreation dance studios because the focus on classical ballet technique is often secondary to winning competitions through acrobatic feats.

Some metropolitan cities have classical jazz studios that teach a specific jazz style, such as those mentioned in chapter 2. These studios usually allow for a methodical progression within the margins of the style, both in the classroom and in advancement.

Combo classes, offered to the youngest students, will frequently include two or more disciplines during a forty-five-minute to one-hour class. The classes can include ballet, tap, and acrobatics (sometimes called tumbling), or ballet, tap, and jazz, or any combination thereof. If young children need to change shoes during the class, from tap to ballet shoes, for example, it takes quite a bit of time. The teacher or the assistant must help each student. These classes are usually fun for the students, but they contain little content that actually prepares the students for continued study.

Teachers in these studios also vary. Some received their training in the studio where they teach, and the studio deems them capable to teach the beginner levels. Others have had professional experience or successful dance careers. Their training and experience are as important as the means they use to deliver the information to the students. It is not unusual for the jazz teacher to also teach ballet. Again, observation of classes can help in your decision to enroll your child. It is important that the teachers properly warm up the students, at all levels, before introducing more challenging or advanced steps. A class that begins with large jumps, intense stretches, or prolonged balance on one leg is not recommended.

Each family must personally decide when to start a child on the jazz track. Some think jazz is for older dancers, as some of the dances and movements can be interpreted as sexually suggestive. Others see them as cute and nonthreatening for a student they consider too young to understand the meaning or feeling behind the movements. The decision is up to you.

Classes are offered for every age group, and there will be performance opportunities within the school and on the competition circuit. If you choose to have your child compete, be prepared to pay for entry fees and costumes. Each dance has its own costume, and each dance that is registered in competition has a separate registration fee. Some schools will be more aggressive in the number of competitions they attend annually. Find out what the school requires in case your child is accepted into one of the competition groups. Make sure it fits within the capability of your family's schedule and finances.

Tap is sometimes included in competitions. Tap classes may be offered as part of the competitors' required class schedule. It should also be available as a class in and of itself. Once again, a good teacher is the key to success in tap.

Acrobatics and gymnastics need to be heavily supervised in a properly equipped room complete with safety mats. Spotting equipment and spotters (people who stand nearby to help participants avoid injury) should be present to help students when they attempt new feats. New movements should only be introduced when they are within the strength and ability of the student.

Hip-hop classes are another discipline that can be enjoyed by all ages. The music needs to be carefully chosen for each age group, as rap music, which is often used, can take on many forms with a variety of lyrics that may be considered inappropriate for children. As with any dance form, hip-hop classes should begin with a warm-up to avoid injury.

Modern Dance Studios

Modern dance studios may not be easy to find outside of metropolitan or university areas. These studios sometimes offer creative dance classes for the youngest students. Creative dance is an excellent alternative for the child who is not ready for the more disciplined approach of the pre-ballet class. Ballet may also be offered at modern dance studios, but it is usually intended to support the development of the students in the modern dance discipline. Frequently, it is not as rigorous as ballet classes found in classical ballet studios.

Classical modern techniques, such as Graham, Limón, and Cunningham, combine with ballet to form the basis of many professional training programs. The influences of these techniques are also present in many current choreographic works. The term *contemporary* provides a more accurate description of the modern dance classes offered by most dance schools today. *Contemporary* describes the eclectic nature of the form. Studios that offer modern dance classes often have classes ranging from creative movement to classical modern styles, to postmodern techniques, to somatic practices. Contemporary or modern dance classes are generally structured to help children develop their own expressive style of movement and to build self-confidence through those movements, rather than to teach a codified technique that develops specific coordination needed to execute specific steps. Since the classes vary significantly according to the style and training of the teacher, it is best to try them out before deciding which style is right for your child.

Class Sizes

As with school classes, too many students in a dance class will hinder progress. Even so, small classes or individual instruction are not essential to the student's progress. Students usually benefit from dancing in a medium-size group. Class size should be in accordance with the size of the studio and the age of the students. Older students will learn well in a class of around twenty-five students. Younger, beginning, or pre-ballet students need smaller classes of fifteen to twenty students. These numbers allow for individualized instruction and attention, which help students develop good technique and progress to the next level.

Master Classes

Master classes, classes given by well known guest teachers or working professionals, can be quite large. Master classes try to give as many students as possible access to the guest and the information that guest has to share on a one-time or infrequent basis. These teachers usually come at a high price, so the school needs high number of attendees to cover the expense. In order to fully benefit from these classes, students need to be mature enough to grasp the information without personal attention. Master classes often give aspiring teen dancers the motivation they need to continue sacrificing social opportunities and working hard to improve their dancing.

—⁓—

At the start of a master class given by dancer David Hallberg, he cautioned the dancers, "You can't change your technique in the next hour-and-a-half class. Know why you are here and what you want to accomplish."

—⁓—

Floors

Raised or sprung floors are ideal for dance study. They afford flexibility, or "give," which is particularly important when jumping. This give helps absorb the impact of the dancer's body, which reduces stress and long-term injuries to bones and joints. Wooden floors are acceptable as long as they have not been laid over cement. They should be un-waxed and smooth. A material called Marley is often placed over the floor surface. It is a black or gray rubberlike material that can be taped into place over the existing floor. It provides a smooth surface and reduces slipping. A studio should never have cement flooring or cement directly under the wood or Marley flooring. Over time, dancing and jumping on cement will cause needless injury to dancers. During your observation of classes, make note or ask about the type of flooring in the studio, remembering the best floor structure for dancing is a sprung floor. These floors enhance performance and greatly reduce injuries.

Accompanist

If you find a studio that uses an accompanist for classes, you are very lucky indeed. It is a special skill not easily found in a musician, and an accompanist is an added expense for the school. Live music offers extensive benefits. Live accompaniment allows the teacher a freedom not available when using pre-recorded music. Accompanists can vary tempos, add accents, and emphasize the feeling of the music to fit the exercises and the ability of the students. The instructor directs the accompanists. Occasionally, during summer programs, the musicians teach music classes specifically for dancers' needs. This is an additional benefit for your student.

Viewing Classes

Some studios have large viewing windows where parents can watch classes at all times. Other studios only allow parents

Viewing windows for parents
Photo by Lynn Battenberg, courtesy of Bender
Performing Arts, Phoenix, Arizona

to observe classes at certain times of the year. There are pros and cons to both scenarios.

The ability to watch a class anytime allows a nervous parent to check on their students. This can put a parent at ease, but it can have the unfortunate consequence of allowing parents to distract the students or make them self-conscious. With the youngest students, whose attention spans are developing, seeing a parent, even through a window, can distract their attention away from the teacher and class instruction or make them want to leave the class.

Parents who view classes regularly may develop the thought that they are qualified to give the student corrections at home. Some parents try to give advice during class through gestures. Parents have gone as far as to assume that by watching they became experts on what should and should not be taught in class. They will approach the teachers with their "advice." Such actions are never appropriate; they go against the basic rules of respect in all dance studios.

Many studios set aside designated parent viewing days a few times a year. This practice allows parents to see the class structure and the progress of their students in the context of class, rather than only seeing them onstage at recitals.

—◊◊—

I once had a parent tell me after a class observation day that she now understood why we only allowed viewing a few times a year. She said it was such a delight to see her child's progress from the last time parents were allowed to watch. She said she might not have detected the changes had she been watching weekly. Another parent, whose young child had spent the whole class waving at her mother, also understood why opportunities to view classes were limited.

—◊◊—

Changing Studios

If you have been at the same studio for several years, changing to another studio can be a sticky situation. As a parent, your job is to do what you feel is best for your student and proceed as needed. The studio has many concerns, as well. When a student leaves, the studio loses income. Most schools pay salaries to the directors, teachers, and accompanists. Company schools may also contribute to paying company expenses.

If your student has been at the school for a long time, that school may also feel a sense of ownership, pride, involvement, success, or accomplishment in your child's progress. Your decision to leave may cause resentment and thoughts of betrayal and ingratitude. On the other side, as many teachers and directors know, with some difficult students, the school may feel relief at not having to work with a child who is uncooperative, inattentive, or uninterested in dance.

Be aware of the owner's and director's perspective of your decision to leave their studio so that the disappointment, which often shows itself as anger, does not come as a surprise. Be prepared for a range of reactions from sincere best wishes to outright hostility.

Some directors will not be placated, no matter how civil and thankful you are as you prepare to leave. It is still in your best interest to leave gracefully, understanding that although they may not be happy at that moment, these are the people who have prepared your child to this point. A nice note or flowers, if there has been no prior animosity between you and the school, would be an appropriate expression of your appreciation for all the hours they have spent training your child. A note to say you are leaving and to thank them for their time, regardless of the reasons for your departure, will set you firmly on the high road.

Parents and students occasionally leave a studio because they feel their talent is not being recognized. It is true that some teachers respond to and encourage certain "types" of dancers more than others. (A "type" may have long legs, red hair, long feet, brown skin, or any number of other qualities.) If this is the case and your student is not that type, you may want to look elsewhere for instruction. If, on the other hand, the teacher or studio is known for excellent training, students may still benefit by learning to incorporate all corrections and information into their own development, even if instruction is not personalized to them.

—⁓—

One student who studied at the same studio for ten years and performed principal roles in the school's performances chose to leave the school as the competition for the lead roles increased. She attended a rival dance school that had a student company associated with it and that she thought would afford her more performance opportunities. She had the misfortune of being the first long-term student to leave her original school. The directors did not handle the situation with aplomb. Hurt feelings abounded on both sides.

—⁓—

If you receive negative or discouraging feedback from two or three teachers, it may be best to accept that feedback as truth. For example, if several different teachers tell a student that the student does not work hard (a catch-all phrase for a student who does not take corrections and apply them or who may not have the ability to push his or her body to the point required to improve in dance), it may be true. Some students can change or grow into an understanding of how to work, using the corrections they receive to improve their dancing; other students, for a variety of reasons, cannot accurately apply corrections.

—⁓—

Parents have told me on numerous occasions how much their child loves dancing, saying that the child dances all the time around the house. Yet, in class I see none of the enthusiasm. Dance students have to enjoy the discipline of class and must take responsibility for their behavior and work ethic fairly early in their studies.

—⁓—

Precautions

Some schools and directors put the financial well-being of the dance school or their reputation ahead of the needs of the students. Be cautious not to allow this to happen to your student. This might take the form of requiring students to participate in the studio performance or in the school's summer program for the financial benefit of the school.

As addressed later, students should not attend residential dance programs alone away from home until they are old enough and mature enough to benefit and handle the responsibilities these programs require. Younger children are often better off when accompanied by a parent or guardian. However, if your child is accepted into a reputable summer program when he or she is mature enough to attend, study outside your home studio could contribute to your child's progress.

Sometimes students can be coerced into participating in competitions their family cannot afford. The student is responsible for paying for travel, registration, and costumes. Coaching and choreography fees are usually paid directly to studio staff. Involvement in these events may benefit a student, but summer programs and competitions are not mandatory steps on the road to a successful dance career.

Keep in mind that a school's inability to help families through every situation does not necessarily mean the school does not care. It could mean that it cannot give the special attention your child needs and still accommodate the rest of the students. Nevertheless, it might indicate that it is time to find a new studio. Consider enrolling your child in another school or perhaps he or she may need a break from dance.

Checklist for Selecting a Studio

1. Does it offer the types of dance you want at the intensity you want?

   Modern, Ballet, Jazz, Tap, Hip-Hop, Stretch, Lyrical, Pointe, Men's classes Partnering

2. Does it have more than one level of each type of dance? Beginner 1 and 2; Intermediate 1 and 2; Advanced 1 and 2

3. Does it have different age level classes for each style of dance taught?

4. Is it accessible enough to your home or school to allow you to attend on time?

5. Questions for the director:

   a) What are the fees?

   b) Is a payment schedule available?

   c) What is the syllabus or style of teaching? Does the studio have a syllabus that spans from beginners to advanced in the different disciplines offered?

   d) What, if any, parental participation expectations are there? (For instance, will you be required to chaperone students in the dressing room during rehearsals or at the recital?)

   e) Are parents allowed to view classes? When and how often?

   f) What performance opportunities are offered? What performance fees are involved? Is participation in the performance mandatory?

g) What classes are offered for your child's age?

h) What are the class sizes?

i) What is the school's philosophy; does it have a mission statement? Is there a written discipline policy?

j) How does the school address bullying?

k) Is a dress code, hair code, or shoe brand required for class?

l) Is there an audition process? Placement class? Is a signed contract required to ensure payment? What are the details of the contract?

m) What experience and background do the teachers in your child's level have? What about teachers of more advanced levels?

n) Do the classes have the same teacher(s) throughout the year?

o) What access do parents have to the teachers? What is the process for discussing concerns?

p) Is there live music or pre-recorded music?

q) When is the school closed for holidays? For vacations? For weather? How will parents and students be notified of closings? Is there a master calendar available when you register?

Additional questions for competition studios:

r) At what age can students compete?

s) Must they be part of a group or company to participate?

t) Must they audition for the company, or is participation by class?

u) How many competitions does the studio participate in each year?

v) What is the average cost?

w) Are classes offered for those who don't want to
compete? Are they taught by the same teachers
as classes for students who do compete?

x) What are the schedules for those students who
compete and those who do not?

IV

Teachers

Selecting a dance school with knowledgeable teachers is important for many reasons. Chief among these is that when people decide to learn a new skill, they should learn how to do it correctly. A good teacher is essential.

Students of the School at Jacob's Pillow Ballet Program.
Virginia Johnson, artistic director of Dance Theater of Harlem,
instructs students. Courtesy of Jacob's Pillow Dance Festival
Photo by Kristi Pitsch

Qualifications

Teachers who understand the ways the body works and the stages of growth and development can help students avoid injuries. Their knowledge of when to give students specific stretches or strengthening exercises for future skills will help protect students' growing bodies.

Another important reason to select a dance school with knowledgeable staff is to support your child's dreams. Parents do not want to be responsible for broken dreams. A student who starts with an unskilled teacher may end up with deficiencies in training, which may later prevent that student from pursuing a career in dance.

—◊—

When I was dancing, I had peers who came from studios where they were considered "top dog" only to audition and find out that they lacked strength and the basic technique required of professional dancers. All the dance and acrobatic tricks in the world do not make up for a lack of accurate execution of basic dance techniques. Thirty-two fouetté turns (a turn made famous by the black swan in Swan Lake) on a bent knee will not get anyone into a reputable dance troupe. Encouraging students to perform complex maneuvers before they master preliminary movements is dangerous and irresponsible, yet it happens in various studios across the country.

—∿—

All dance teachers, no matter the discipline, should have a clear understanding of the dance form they are sharing with students. They must themselves have had years of study with competent teachers, respect and commitment to the art form, and passion to pass on knowledge and a love of dance.

Dance teachers should have a history of performance experiences in addition to those in recital settings. They need not have had professional careers; their experience could include performances with civic and other nonprofessional companies or community theater groups. Training with more than one studio or teacher is also important, as that experience exposes the teacher to a variety of personalities, curricula, and styles of dance. A degree in dance, certification from a dance education program, or a lengthy dance career can, but does not always, produce a competent dance teacher. Credentials and performance experience do not give a complete picture, so parents must do further research.

—∿—

One year, a large number of students transferred into my class. The parents explained that a teacher from another studio was putting their children, ages six through eight years old, on pointe. To "go on pointe" means allowing students to wear pointe shoes and dance literally on their toes. To put a student on pointe before ten years old is, by conventional wisdom (not to mention physical readiness), too soon. Some studios promote students to pointe to appease parents; others simply need to fill class rosters at the risk of damaging students' feet. In this situation, I was most disturbed by the fact that this particular teacher had a certificate from one of the top teacher-education programs in the country. In other words, she should have known better. This is an example of why no one should depend solely on how a teacher looks on paper but must look further into the classroom and curriculum used at the school.

—⁂—

Beginning-level dance classes, including pre-dance programs such as pre-ballet, creative movement, and combo classes, should not be throw-away classes taught by a novice teacher. This level requires a specific instructional skill; it requires a teacher who can properly instruct the students on musicality, discipline, and respect for the art form. The teacher must have an understanding of age-appropriate discipline and physical ability, combined with patience and a pleasant presentation. Otherwise, the class is simply an expensive babysitting situation.

Students in a Pre-ballet class at the Washington School of Ballet
Photo provided by Media4Artist, Theo Kossenas, courtesy of
Washington Ballet and the Washington School of Ballet

A teacher for the intermediate and upper levels needs patience of a different kind to work with teenagers. These students' changing bodies and transition into puberty add an emotional aspect that, although it cannot be catered to, needs to be taken into consideration. The classes at this level become stricter and more disciplined as the teacher expects more of the dancer. A teacher must be able to give meaningful corrections. "That is wrong" is not an acceptable correction, unless followed by further instruction and feedback as to what specifically is wrong and how the student can correct the error.

The requirements of the advanced-level teacher include the ability to polish the dancer's technique in preparation for a higher-level of performance. At this level, a teacher's experience working on the styles and nuances of choreography becomes of great value. This is the level at which the student receives artistic polish.

As in an academic classroom, every teacher is not a good fit for every student. A good match between student and teacher is especially important when the students are young. Before placing your child in a school, ask to view the teacher at work. Many schools have limits on viewing classes your students are attending but do not have a policy against watching the class that your child plans to enter. These arrangements should be made in advance out of respect for the teacher, the director, and the other participants in the class. If parents are not allowed to watch a class prior to enrolling their child in the program, review other policies in greater detail and seriously consider whether the school's policy toward parents will be a good fit for your family.

Watch how the teacher presents information to the students and how the students react to the teacher. Is there respect, fear, or anger? Mutual respect is desirable. A teacher does not need to yell, scream, berate, or embarrass students. That is not to say that an unfocused child will not try the patience of the teacher. Some yelling during class and rehearsals should be expected, mostly so the teacher may be heard over the crowd, but also because emotions run high before performances. Teachers should never use obscenities, name-calling, or humiliation.

Students will be pushed hard to work, but a teacher should never do anything to harm a child, mentally or physically. Teachers should not give exercises that are harmful to joints or muscles. That being said, parents need to understand that most ballet steps, as well as other dance steps, can be quite unnatural to what the body does on a daily basis. They demand a high degree of effort. The key is age-appropriate exercises and an understanding of the student's skills and limitations. These elements will be familiar to any teacher worth his or her salt.

Student stretching to increase turn out
Photo by Lynn Battenberg, courtesy of Scottsdale
School of Ballet, Scottsdale, Arizona

Tears may occasionally occur in the dance studio, but a student who is constantly crying needs an opportunity to address what is bothering him or her. Whether the student puts the stress on himself or herself or feels it is coming from the teacher, these feelings should not be ignored. A studio's response to students and parents in these situations may be a reason a child should remain with the studio or leave it.

Male Teachers of Young Men

You need not worry about a gay male dance teacher being inappropriate with your son any more than you should worry about a straight teacher preying on your son. *Homosexuality* and *pedophilia* are not synonymous. *A homosexual or a gay person* refers to someone's sexual preference for the same gender; it alone should not be considered deviant or dangerous. *Pedophilia* occurs when an adult has a sexual attraction to children; this condition is accompanied by behavior that is dangerous, psychologically and physically, for children. This can be a heterosexual or homosexual attraction. Pedophilia is no more prevalent in a dance studio than in society in general.

Of course, if a teacher of either gender behaves in a way that makes a child uncomfortable, that behavior is worth discussing with the child and the teacher. Keep in mind that corrections will include a certain amount of touching to manipulate the student's body.

—∞—

After I substituted for another teacher's class, a boy, about ten years old, came up to me and explained that he did not like being touched during corrections. The touching had included manipulation of his foot to show the proper stretch of the arch, as well as adjustment to his spine to get him "over his legs" for balance. The touching had been nothing out of the norm, in the dance environment, but it had made the child uncomfortable. I am sure his parents had talked to him about standing up for himself and the dangers of bad touching. After thanking him for his candor, I explained to him that while there are indeed limits, the touching used to correct dancers was for his benefit and part of the learning process. If this level of physical contact is uncomfortable for your child, the dance studio is probably not the best place for him or her. Dance is not the same as a classroom education, where most touching is not allowed. Touch is often necessary to help the student understand how to place the body or how to implement the correction.

—ɯ—

Teacher and School Director Kee Juan Han instructs
a boys' class at the Washington School of Ballet.
Photo provided by Media4Artist, Theo Kossenas, courtesy
of Washington Ballet and the Washington School of Ballet

Physical Corrections

As with all touching, there is good and bad, appropriate and inappropriate, contact even in the dance studio. Corrections in dance are intended to call attention to expected forms and ways to correct mistakes. It is part of good teaching to take the leg and rotate it to help the student understand the range of turn out and the location of turn-out muscles. A

Natalia Magnicaballi, teacher, corrects a student
during class.
Photo by Michael Cook, courtesy of Tempe Dance, Tempe, Arizona

touch to the tummy to remind the student to pull up and a tap on the shoulder as a reminder to keep it down are all within a dance teacher's normal behavior.

However, if this or other touching makes your child feel uncomfortable, it must be addressed immediately. Talk to your child, and then talk with the teacher about how your child is interpreting the touching. If you go to the teacher nonjudgmentally, without accusations but with sincere concern for your student and a desire to clear up any misunderstandings, you can usually find a solution together.

—⟋⟍⟍—

One parent approached me to let me know that her adopted child had experienced abuse before the adoption. Because of this, when giving corrections, I was careful about where I put my hand to emphasize the correction. I was glad the parent had shared this information with me, as it allowed the child to continue studying dance with comfort and confidence, eventually becoming a capable dancer.

—⟋⟍⟍—

Private Lessons

Private lessons are needed only for specific purposes. Students gain an advantage when they learn to incorporate information and corrections in a class setting. The majority of professional dancing takes place in a group, whether it occurs in a music video, Broadway, or the corps de ballet.

A private lesson can help a student catch up after an injury or illness, allowing that student to move at his or her own level of capability and avoid being reinjured. (With a willing teacher, this may sometimes be accomplished in a class setting).

Students involved in competitions in which they will perform a solo often use private lessons, or coaching, to polish their performance.

If your studio closes for an extended period during the summer (perhaps four weeks), and there are no other classes available at the appropriate level, you might supplement training with private lessons.

Communication with the Teacher

Speaking to your child's teacher can be a very delicate task. Although presumably well schooled in dance, not all dance teachers are familiar with stages of child development or ways of interacting with parents. Many have not raised children of their own, so their understanding of the needs of a family may be minimal.

Add to that what is politely called "artistic temperament," and the need to select words carefully becomes clear.

Before approaching a teacher for a conference, parents need to know the policy of the school; some directors do not allow parents to speak with the teachers directly or without an administrative representative present. Others merely ask that parents schedule a time with the teacher so as not to disrupt the teaching schedule. It is never good to catch a teacher between tightly scheduled classes. What may be a convenient time for you may not be convenient for the teacher and may not allow sufficient time for thoughtful consideration of your concerns.

Approach the conversation from a positive point of view. For example, say, "My child has mentioned something to me, and I want to better understand what may have happened in the class," or, "I have some concerns about my child's progress and wonder if you could help me to address them." Introduce the subject in a nonthreatening way.

—⚍—

After observing a class, a mother approached me to ask why I had not corrected her daughter when she clearly was doing something incorrectly. I explained that I had corrected her child on other issues. The child dutifully accepted and applied the corrections. Considering the child's age and level of the class, I felt that she had accomplished enough and adding more corrections would simply overwhelm her and she wouldn't hold on to what she was already accomplishing.

—⚍—

It is not unheard of for a student to misinterpret a teacher's correction or statement. Teachers often use exaggerations or metaphors to emphasize a point they are trying to make. Sometimes students project their sensitivities, inhibitions, or insecurities onto innocent corrections. Approach any perceived problem with calmness; more times than not, the teacher means no malice and is unaware of the misunderstanding or hurt feelings.

—∞—

A teacher who was attempting to encourage a student to hold the stomach in said, "I don't want to see your breakfast. Hold your tummy in." The parents came in to complain that their six-year-old no longer wanted to eat breakfast. The teacher had no intention of causing strife in the house or setting the stage for an eating disorder. I have used similar terminology but have never had the same reaction. Each child is different; allow the teacher the benefit of the doubt and believe that the teacher is doing his or her best to educate your child in dance. Occasionally, misunderstandings may occur.

—⟋⟍—

It is never appropriate for parents, on behalf of their child, to request or demand parts in a performance or advancement from class to class. Parents may calmly ask for an explanation if they do not see their child progressing through the program and feel the child is not being challenged. Your goal should be for your child's teacher or the studio director to understand your concerns without causing hurt feelings on either side. Parents deserve to have their concerns addressed. Instructors deserve to be treated with respect.

Teachers should be able to explain their teaching progression and discipline style, but they should not have to defend themselves after every class. Assuming parents have seen no signs of problems in the studio, parents need to trust the professionals and allow them to do their job; otherwise, your child probably should not be enrolled at that school.

Checklist for Observing Classes
Classroom Management/Environment

1. How does the teacher address or greet students in class?
   a. Does the teacher acknowledge the students individually or as a group, or does he or she start class without acknowledging students?
2. Are the students attentive to the teacher?
   a. The level of focus will vary with the age of the class, but all levels should demonstrate respect for the teacher and accept corrections graciously.
3. Can the teacher manage the class?
   a. The class should not sound like a playground.
   b. Students should be on task.
   c. Students should remain in the class, leave only with the teacher's permission (barring emergencies), and avoid entering and exiting the studio between exercises.
4. How does the teacher address disruption in the class?
   a. Although strict, is the teacher appropriately respectful to all students?
   b. Is anyone smiling? Within the structure of the class, students should occasionally smile and should enjoy the class.
5. Is there a dress code?
   a. If so, is it followed consistently?
   b. For ballet, are students wearing tights and leotards? Is their hair up?

    c. Jazz and modern dance have a wider variety of acceptable attire and hairstyles, but appropriate shoes in both jazz and tap are necessary.

    d. Hip-hop requires comfortable clothes that allow students to move.

6. Does the teacher dress for class?

    a. Is he or she dressed in attire conducive to movement and demonstration of the steps, including appropriate dance shoes?

    b. Street clothing is not appropriate for teaching dance unless it is an advanced class or an older teacher.

    c. Teachers often wear teaching skirts or exercise pants for class, and appropriate shoes are necessary. (A teacher need not wear pointe shoes to teach a pointe class.)

7. How does the teacher give corrections?

    a. Does he or she give corrections in a manner appropriate to the age of the students?

    b. Does the teacher give corrections generally, or personally to different students? Students need both to learn.

    c. Does the teacher give personal corrections in a nondegrading way?

Class Structure

1. Does the teacher give exercises that allow students to properly warm up?

    a. All styles of dance have warm-ups, which can include slow floor stretching, ballet barre exercises, or slow set tapping exercises.

    b. Teachers should never encourage students to begin a class with large jumps, kicks, or advanced moves.

2. Does the class have a reasonable sequence, which includes warm-up, strengthening exercises, and dance execution?

    a. This is where a school syllabus may be important.

    b. There are certain exercises that students should learn at each level. They are added in each section of the class and include skills from warm-ups to leaps.

3. Is the musical accompaniment appropriate for the students' age, the style of dance, and the exercises?

    a. Are jazz or hip-hop music lyrics appropriate for the ages in the class?

    b. Is classical music the main type used in ballet class?

    c. Music is not always used in tap classes.

    d. Does the recorded song give instructions to the children, or does the teacher give the instructions? (Instructions should come from the teacher.)

V

Cost and Clothing

Tuition

The costs of dance education are significant, but this should not hinder an earnest child from participating. Scholarships awarded by studios, foundations, or civic clubs may defray costs. These scholarships may be need or talent based. You may find a studio that offers free or income-based classes. For the experienced dancer looking for extra classes, this is great, but a beginning dance student should make sure that all classes are high quality.

—⟋⟍—

Several dancers in some of America's top ballet companies trained for years though funds awarded by the Boys and Girls Clubs of America.

—⟋⟍—

Without scholarships, total costs for classes will grow as the hours of study increase, but that usually means that the cost per class will decrease. Additional costs for a dedicated dancer may include summer programs, competitions, and private study. These costs can propel fees exponentially. These additional courses of study or performance each have their benefits, but they are not the only ways to a successful dance career.

Summer programs often include a combination of intensive study and summer-camp activities. There are numerous programs offered throughout the country that target a variety of price ranges and ability levels. Full and partial scholarships are available for many of these programs. Parents will want to spend time learning about the different programs and evaluating what will fit the needs, interests, and abilities of their child. Some programs require an audition; others require a photo or audition tape, and still others are open to anyone interested in attending who has the money to pay tuition.

Scholarships are available for most summer programs and home studios, but they are not abundant. Companies associated with dance, such as specialty-floor suppliers and dance-clothing manufacturers, sometimes offer scholarships.

Competitions are a pricey addition to a dance education. The benefits are mixed and will be discussed in later chapters. Some prizes include cash, but they do not always cover the costs associated with participation; also, the competition may award a few scholarships for upcoming competitions. With those exceptions, costs of competitions lay solely on the dancers and their family. Choreography, private coaching, travel, lodging, entry fees, and costuming are all required for solo competitions. If your student participates as part of a team at a studio, annual team fees may cover some of the costs. See chapter 8 for more information about competitions and summer programs.

Clothing

Similar to the price of daily wear, the cost for dance attire varies greatly depending on the quality, style, and brand of the dance clothing purchased. It can be reasonably priced or expensive. A leotard for women should fit snugly, like a one-piece bathing suit. Leotards come in a variety of colors and styles, including long sleeved, short sleeved, low back, and turtleneck. Some studios have a dress code and require specific styles at different levels. Different studios may have different dress codes.

Tights are worn on the legs. Underpants are not worn under women's tights and leotards; they are not necessary, and dancers should never wear them under a costume, as they may show and usually detract from smooth body lines. If necessary, students may wear dance trunks between the skin and a costume. They are tight fitting and are available in colors that will match the dancer's skin color.

Tights need to be washed in warm, soapy water after each use. They may be hand-washed and should never be put in the dryer.

Dance skirts come in different lengths and styles, and some schools consider them part of the dance uniform for certain classes. A student may wear a short skirt, when the school allows it. A skirt that falls above the knee is appropriate for character class, and dancers often wear mid-calf or longer skirts for Flamenco classes.

Dance pants and booty shorts are acceptable attire for jazz, tap, lyrical, and hip-hop classes. There is a wide variety of fits for these items, from tight to baggy, and from very short shorts to longer styles. Tops range from basic T-shirts to more elaborate fitness tops. Students may wear dance pants or shorts over a leotard in lieu of tights in jazz, tap, lyrical, or hip-hop classes.

Schools may allow boys to wear sports clothing at the beginning of their dance training, but, with advancement, they will need to wear either dance pants or tights for men, which are distinctively thicker than those designed for women.

In some instances, men may need to wear leotards under their tights, which have a decidedly different fit from those made for women.

The male dancer wears a dance belt. It is similar to a jock strap in support but goes a step further in that it serves to hide or smooth over the male anatomy under tights. Dance belts resemble thongs and may take some getting used to.

Like underwear for men, dance belts are sized by waist size, and they can be found at specialty dance stores or online. They come in a variety of colors. It is best to get the color closest to that of the dancer's skin.

Depending on the dancer's schedule, he may need more than one dance belt, as it should be laundered after every use. Usually, young boys can get away with tight-fitting underwear until they reach about eleven years old.

—∿—

Unfortunately, dance belts do not behave like underwear. Some boys drive their mothers crazy by putting their underwear on inside out and calling it clean; this will not work with a dance belt.

—∿—

Different Clothing for Different Classes

Acceptable dancewear varies from class to class and studio to studio. Some studios designate leotards of a specific color for each ballet-class level. They may also specify the color of ballet slippers students should wear at each of these levels.

Traditionally, students in ballet classes wear leotards with tights, and ballet slippers that are pink, black, or neutral. At advanced levels, females may wear pointe shoes. Men's ballet-class apparel usually consists of tights, T-shirts, socks, and black or white ballet slippers. As students advance, they may have greater leeway in their dancewear, but only at the teacher's discretion. These requirements aid the teacher in identifying correct and incorrect bodylines. When students all present their bodies in the same costume or class uniform, the teacher can quickly see how they are working their body.

Modern and contemporary classes also require leotards and tights, but usually the tights should be footless to support the

Students in proper ballet attire and hair.
Photo by Michael Cook, courtesy of Tempe Dance, Tempe, Arizona

dance form's predilection toward training and performing bare footed.

Jazz classes may require form-fitting clothing, but they also allow a variety of style and color options compared to ballet class requirements. Shorts, dance pants, and form-fitting T-shirts are often acceptable in jazz classes. Bright colors and patterned leotards and tights may be allowed.

Tap and hip-hop, as well as ethnic dance classes, do not require the same strict uniform guidelines seen in ballet and modern dance classes. They only require comfortable clothing that does not restrict movement. You may see baggy pants, shorts, T-shirts, and tight-fitting exercise tops in these classes. Hats, scarves, and ponytails are also options.

Different Hairstyles for Different Classes

There is a purpose for different hair requirements for different dance classes. The "ballet bun," which has often caused ballet students to be referred to as ""bunheads," is a well -known and widely recognized style. The hair is pulled back and off the face to provide the least distraction for both the teacher and the student during class.

For dancers on stage, most ballets also require hair to be up and away from the face. This contributes to the view of the dancer's face and the line of the body. It also reduces the chance of hair hitting a partner during turns or lifts. Certain ballets require the dancer's hair to be worn down to emphasize an emotion or a part of the story. In one of the most famous of these scenes, from the ballet *Giselle*, the

The ballet bun
Photo courtesy of Scottsdale School of Ballet, Scottsdale, Arizona

ballerina, lets her hair down as she begins her decline into insanity. Modern and contemporary dance often allow free-flowing hair, as it adds to the earthy expression of the dance form. For performance purposes, modern dancers often pull the front of their hair back into a clip, opening up the face but allowing the rest of the hair to flow freely behind them.

—⁓—

When speaking with new dance parents, I always stress that, "Dad had to do it today" is not an acceptable excuse for a child showing up with-

out a proper bun for ballet class. If you have a female dancer in your family, all members who may be in charge of getting your dancer to class must know the proper clothing, shoes, and hairstyle. It truly takes a village to raise a dancer.

—∞—

Jazz and tap classes often permit a variety of hairstyles, including hair completely loose, in ponytails, and in softly put-together buns. Acceptable hairstyles for jazz class are determined by what the teacher allows. This is also true for hip-hop dance classes.

Dance Shoes

Purchase dance shoes at a dance supply store rather than at a discount store, department store, or other store that may stock them. The shoes are more likely to fit properly when fitted by a clerk who is familiar with the process, the variety of shoes available, and the features of each type. It is acceptable to fit your growing child with shoes that provide slight room for growth. *Slight* is the key word, as oversized shoes can hinder both progress and grace.

The shoes in the dance supply stores are, in fact, better quality than those sold in most department stores and other non-dance supply outlets. The materials used are of better quality, and the shoes fit the feet in a superior way. This facilitates proper use of the foot. Ballet slippers, for example, should mold to the dancer's foot and show off its arch and lines. Discount ballet slippers are rarely able to do this. So much in dance is about the foot's correct movements on the ground and in the air, and the line the foot helps create with the leg. The support a shoe gives is very important to a dancer of any age.

The soft leather used in ballet slippers and jazz shoes conforms to the shape of the foot and allows the dancer to learn how to use the foot without fighting the shoe. Some of the shoes sold in discount stores are of stiff leather and, rather than conforming to the foot, actually pull away from it, creating an unattractive effect that does not allow the dancer to succeed in their efforts to show they are working to stretch their foot properly.

Jazz shoes
Photo courtesy of Bender Performing Arts, Phoenix, Arizona

Certain kinds of dance shoes, if still in good condition, may be handed down to siblings or other dance students. Soft ballet slippers, jazz, and tap shoes may all be used again, but only if they fit well. Giving a younger sibling shoes that are too big will impede the skills the sibling can accomplish. Shoes must fit appropriately in length and width. Leather shoes should fit like a glove, close to the foot, with no more than a quarter inch of extra length at the big toe.

Pointe shoes, once worn, should never be worn by another dancer. Since this is one of the most expensive purchases a dancer makes, and the length of use is limited, it is a sad truth. Pointe shoes must be fitted specifically to the dancer's foot by a professional. Then, the break-in process begins. This process allows the shoe to conform to the needs of one particular dancer and one particular foot. Even if the handed-down shoe looks nearly new, it has the potential to cause a student to improperly use her foot, and, in the worst case, that may cause injury.

A Word about Pointe Shoes

Finally getting pointe shoes is a young ballet student's dream, but it is often one of the most confusing events for a parent. There are many rules and traditions associated with the care and maintenance of the shoe itself. The costs associated with the shoes, which have the shortest lifespan of any other dance product, can come as a shock to parents.

For an advanced dancer, even the relatively inexpensive elastics, pins, and hairnets have a longer lifespan than a pointe shoe.

Next to a qualified teacher, the pointe-shoe fitting is the most important thing when taking ballet to this advanced

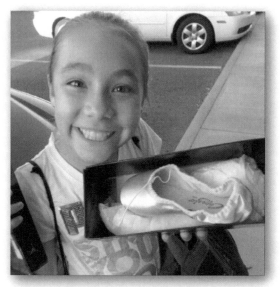

First pair of pointe shoes
Photo courtesy of Chris Lee

level. High-quality dance supply stores have people on staff who are trained to do the fitting. Teachers from a studio may schedule a visit to the store en masse and oversee the fitting themselves. When your student obtains her first pair of pointe shoes, there must be someone present who knows what they are doing.

Both elastic and ribbon are used to secure the shoe on the foot. Traditionally, the elastic is sewn on the outside of the shoe in the back by the heel, on either side of the back seam, at varying distance apart, depending on the dancer's preference and the teacher's instructions. Ribbons are sewn onto the sides of the shoe. The heel of the shoe should be folded forward; the ribbons should be sewn on the inside of the shoe in the space where the heel overlaps the side of the shoe. Teachers may have certain tricks they pass on to their students that have worked for them.

—w—

A teacher had her students sew their ribbons on each side of the shoe, varying slightly so that when the ribbons were tied, they lay flatter across the arch of the foot. I had not been taught to do this, but it seemed like a very good idea.

—w—

Students just beginning on pointe can usually keep the same pair of shoes for several weeks or months, as at this level, the wear and tear is minimal. The more advanced student may go through a pair or more a week.

Should you feel the need for more information about proper pointe shoe fitting, training, technique, and foot care, there are several books available on these topics. **The Pointe Book is in its second printing by authors, Jancie Barringer and Sara Schlesinger. *The Dancer's Foot Book,* by Dr. Terry L. Spilken is also available as of this writing.**

Dance Bags

All dancers need a dance bag, but its contents will differ with a student's age.

A young student's dance bag will contain dance shoes, whether tap, ballet, or jazz shoes. It may contain an extra set of dance clothing, as clothes might get spilled on or torn before class. A pair of socks may come in handy if shoes become too tight or a blister appears. With the teacher's approval, students may wear them for class in lieu of shoes. (This should not be done regularly because socks are slippery.)

For students with long hair, extra hair supplies are essential. Students should assemble brush, comb, elastics, headbands, clips, bobby pins, and hairpins (yes, those are different) in a cosmetic case and add that to the dance bag.

Dance bags
Photo by Lynn Battenberg,
courtesy of Bender Performing
Arts, Phoenix, Arizona

A refillable water bottle needs to correlate to the size and effort of the student. A five-year-old taking a one-hour class does not need more than a sip or two of water during class. Any more than that and the student will need trips out of class to the bathroom. This is not ideal for the learning process.

The next level of dancer will not only add to their dance bag, but often carry a backpack as well to accommodate schoolwork, which, in many cases, the student will do between classes, while waiting for classes to begin, or after classes while waiting for parents. Dancers can add leg warmers and sweaters to the bag to keep warm before class and between classes. Students will add different dancewear depending on which classes he or she is taking and the dress code for each class.

Girls will want to pack an emergency kit for menses to keep in the bag at all times. When pointe classes begin, students will need rolls of tape for protecting toes, as well as toe pads, lamb's wool, or the dancer's choice of foot protection.

All dancers will want Band-Aids and possibly corn pads, which can protect a blister from further distress.

As the dancer progresses, the bag will begin to include choice stretching aids such as TheraBands or rollers to relax the foot. Different-sized balls can be used to ease tight muscles in the back or legs. Tennis balls inside a sock are not uncommon in dancers' bags. Ointments for sore muscles and Ace bandages can be carried for backup.

At a certain point in their physical development, students will need hygienic aids, so deodorants as well as lightly scented powder will be helpful. Strong perfumes or body sprays can overwhelm the studio, especially if everyone has a different and competing scent.

VI

Physical and Emotional Aspects of Dance

Dance Bodies

Body image can be a huge issue among dancers. The studios have walls filled with mirrors and the dance attire fits close to the body. Dance focuses on turning the body into a strong and aesthetically pleasing dance machine.

Fitness is vital to success as a dancer. Simple feats like bending over to touch your toes are easier with a lean body. Jumping and leaping to preferred heights, is easier to attain with a lean body. When one dancer lifts another into the air, a lean body is crucial.

In many dance forms, the lines developed and shown during performance are of great importance. This refers to the literal lines the body can make when executing a variety of dance steps. When looking at a dancer, you can see the line made from the tip of the finger to the stretch of the toe. The line is different in each step, but the cohesiveness is the same. Lines show more clearly on a lean body.

An example of the lines dancers make with their
bodies, from the Washington School of Ballet.
Photo by Media4Artists, Theo Kossenas. Photographs provided
courtesy of Washington Ballet and the Washington School of Ballet

A dancer can develop the body beyond the boundaries of heredity traits by using the body in a specific way during years of training. The muscles become long and lean with the help of strengthening and stretching exercises. It is not unusual to see a short, overweight parent with a long, lean dancer.

When students start comparing their body type to others, problems can arise. Lean does not mean skinny. Most professional dancers are thin, but to perform at their peak, they must maintain a balanced, nutritional diet and proper sleep and rest from a physically challenging schedule.

The idea of the ultra-thin ballet dancer can be traced back to George Balanchine and his muses. Mr. Balanchine is one of the most celebrated twentieth-century choreographers. He was cofounder and artistic director of New York City Ballet. He filled his company with thin, tall dancers, most notably Tanaquil LeClercq and Suzanne Farrell, who were both naturally long and lean. In an effort to work within this trend, many dancers began the quest to look like these women.

Other forms of dance can be less demanding of specific body types, yet an artistic director or a show choreographer may choose to overlook the most talented dancers in favor of a unified body type for a production. For example, one only needs to look at the Rockettes; if you are less than five feet five inches tall, you have no chance of dancing in the chorus line. Your legs must be as long as the other dancers', and a weight allowance is written into the contract. As you see, many of these demands are out of one's control, predestined by genetic makeup.

Female dancers in the Martha Graham Company tend toward long bodies and strong legs. It is not inconsequential that Ms. Graham also had this body type.

The famous jazz choreographer, Bob Fosse, not unlike Balanchine, had a certain type of muse. His dancers, including his most famous muses, Gwen Verdon and Ann Reinking, had long, beautiful legs and an ability to move within Fosse's distinct style of jazz.

Are Dancers Born or Made?

Like life, dancers arise from a combination of nature and nurture. Certain physical attributes greatly benefit dance.

As mentioned before, flexibility, turn out, and ability to develop a great deal of strength are essential. In ballet, good feet and a natural demi-plié are especially praised. The natural turner is envied in all forms of dance.

Some dancers have taken their traditionally negative attributes and overcome them or turned them into benefits.

Bob Fosse comes to mind, as he struggled with turn out, a rotation of the hips essential to ballet and used often in all dance forms. As a choreographer, he created a style of jazz dance that showcased the turned-in style as part of his distinct technique. It is now a staple in jazz performances and Broadway choreography.

No matter how physically talented, dancers must have the drive to accompany the talent. They must be willing to work hard and accept the challenge of the dance world. Sadly, the hard work and acceptance of the dance world cannot always overcome the lack of natural talent.

Physical Attributes

Your student may be lucky enough to hear that he or she has a physical gift for dancing. The traits that phrase refers to will be similar in most types of dance but may vary slightly.

A ballet dancer who was born with flexibility, turn out, straight or slightly hyperextended legs, and a high arch in the foot will have an easier time tackling the necessary skills. A deep demi-plié (the ability to bend the knees while keeping the heels on the floor) will also help with the jumps needed, especially for the male dancers. A physical propensity for strength and leanness is also vital.

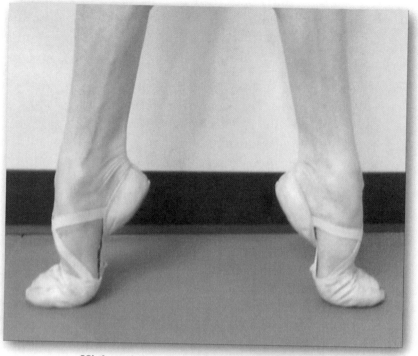

High arches, a benefit to most dance styles
Photo courtesy of Nancy Crowley

A modern dancer will benefit from the physical gifts of a ballet dancer, but those traits are not as rigorously necessary as ballet dictates.

Jazz dancers benefit from flexibility and high arches but also must be able to have a good deal of core body and hip mobility. Jazz dance bodies can vary, but the style is appreciative of lean yet definitely female body types for women and fit, strong masculine body types for men.

All dancers need an understanding of the music. Most can learn this understanding, but occasionally a student is born without it or the ability to develop the skill.

Some forms of dance are more aerobic than others, and these forms will help your child slim down. All forms build stamina, but not all maintain the aerobic level of a Zumba class at a gym.

Some young children who are still carrying some baby fat can easily develop long, lean bodies through dancing. Children who are slightly overweight or obese do not slim down as much as they would in a more aerobic endeavor like swimming or track.

These children have a harder time mastering the skills of flexibility and grace, as their girth can be a deterrent. This trouble can contribute to negative self-image rather than encouragement of fitness. However, students' temperaments and personalities define how they see themselves in the class. Children with a fuller body type can still benefit from all aspects of dance. Regardless of body size, most who study dance will not pursue it professionally, but all can appreciate its benefits.

—⚅—

Professional Ballet Dancer David Hallberg sees the ballet world as discriminatory, in that certain physical attributes do matter. However, he also mentions that dance can help students develop discipline, health, flexibility, movement, and a sense of confidence with performance. Ballet can assist those who want to go to Broadway, which is more accepting of varying body types and which often requires movement no matter one's size.

—⁓—

Diets

Fad and excessive dieting do occur in the dance world; they are dangerous and should be discouraged at all costs. Giving up health to meet a physical ideal will not help students succeed as a dancer.

—⁓—

While a student, one of my fellow dancers decided to keep her weight down by eating mostly carrots. I think the only meal she ate was a light dinner. She lacked nutritional balance, and the palms of her hands turned a distinct shade of orange.

—⁓—

Dancers must learn to take care of themselves. This care includes nutrition, rest, and mental stability.

Diets can be very distinct to the dance professional. Small meals throughout the day may allow a dancer a consistent energy level. Some dancers may fuel up in the morning and evening, preferring to keep little in their stomachs while dancing.

Students, however, especially those still growing and developing, need not restrict their food intake. Their food choices are the key to keeping fit. A balanced diet is important and need not include potato chips or soda. Everything in moderation—a child should not feel hunger. Small snacks of fruit, vegetables, or low-fat granola bars are a good way to keep the stomach from hunger. Though this may surprise some, chocolate milk has been found to be a good source of energy for physical activity. It is available in fat-free and sugar-free varieties.

—∞—

The October/November 2011 issue of Pointe *magazine refers to a study done at the* University of Texas at Austin. *In summary, the study found that nonfat-chocolate-milk drinkers showed improved times while working out, were in better overall shape, and had bodies with more muscle and less fat than those who drank sports drinks.*

—∞—

Eating Disorders

Dance alone does not cause anorexia, an eating disorder in which sufferers starve themselves, however, the focus on trim bodies can contribute. It is therefore important that parents pay close attention to their child's eating habits and weight. **It is equally important that parents not become part of the obsession.**

Parents can help by stocking the fridge with skim milk, fruit, and yogurt. Low-fat snacks such as pudding made with skim milk or frozen yogurt, as opposed to ice cream, are excellent substitutes and will allow growing bodies the sweets they may crave. Balanced diets and proper proportions are the key. Children should not be denied food when hungry; they can receive extra portions of veggies, fruit, and protein in place of carbohydrates or sweets.

If you have concerns about your child's body image, you should talk with the teachers at the studio and consult your doctor. If you need to take action, it is essential that intervention start as soon as possible. Anorexia and another eating disorder, bulimia, can cause irreversible damage to the heart, teeth, and esophagus, among other parts of the body.

Signs of eating disorder can include:

Dramatic weight loss in a short period of time
Obsession with weight
Obsession with calorie intake
Trips to the bathroom after every meal
Excessive use of laxatives
Self-starvation, food restrictions
For girls, loss of menstrual cycle

More complete lists of symptoms can be found by searching the Internet or by consulting a doctor.

Hygiene

When the time is right, help your student understand the need for cleanliness and the use of a deodorant. Young students aren't always gentle with their observations of body odor, and feelings can definitely be bruised.

Students must wear clean workout clothes daily. Parents can help by either participating with the wash or ensuring that students have enough different outfits to last through a week of classes.

When dressing for class or rehearsals, students should use deodorant. They can use a lightly scented powder to help neutralize the perspiration. The powder also works well to keep shoes from becoming too smelly.

If students sweat during class and rehearsals, they can take a hand towel into class to stay the perspiration once it starts dripping.

Hand washing is as essential in the studio as out. Lots of contact during partnering or group dances can spread germs as well as odors.

Menses should not deter a young woman from taking classes. With the thin pads available, they should be invisible even in a leotard. Tampons are easier to use and preferable when the dancer is comfortable with that choice.

VII

Auditions and Performances

Auditions

Auditions are a part of the dance world. As dancers progress in their studies, they often encounter an audition process of one kind or another. Some elite schools audition students to see if they have the skills they desire for admission.

Auditions can be thrilling, and they can be disheartening. One of the hardest things for parents to accept is having no control over the outcome. (And they don't have any control)

A dance studio that has associated dance companies may require students to audition for placement into the program. Schools that participate in competitions can have several levels of companies. Auditions may be repeated annually to allow dancers who are ready to move to a more advanced company or to retain their spot within their company. Even though your child has been in the same studio for years and the staff knows his or her skill level, it is part of the training for dancers who continue into the professional world to learn how to take an audition.

If you notice that the only students getting the solos are related to the staff or those who have made generous donations to the school or company, then it is time to find another school.

Schools also hold auditions for placement in summer dance programs. Different programs will attempt to hold auditions in larger cities that are easily accessible to those who do not live there. Many programs available for students in California and Arizona utilize Los Angeles for an audition site. Likewise, some programs may hold auditions in New York City on the East Coast and then again in Florida, but not in between.

Community theaters, ballet companies, modern dance companies, and charity events that need student dancers for different shows may hold open auditions to fill these roles. These can offer good opportunities and learning experiences. You should not take these commitments lightly, so make sure that any shows you want to join do not conflict with your studio's expectations.

One of the most popular children's auditions is for parts in *The Nutcracker Ballet*, a mainstay of many professional and regional ballet companies. Other winter stories that may also include children's parts are often told through jazz or modern dance.

Students participating in the annual *Nutcracker Ballet*
Photo courtesy of Dorcas Guest Nelson

—⁓—

A student auditioned for a presentation of The Nutcracker *that her studio was putting on. Her mother went to the teacher/choreographer to ask that her daughter be cast in a particular part. The student had been with the studio for many years, and her mother felt she deserved this leading role. The student was a solid dancer, but her skills did not place her in position for leading roles. Her mother set her up for disappointment, to expect the lead role, when she could have simply supported her in the roles she had the skills for, received, and could successfully perform.*

—⁂—

So much can go into the selection for a part. As previously discussed, sometimes a studio desires a specific body type, and if your student doesn't possess that type, no amount of talent will get him or her the role.

The students must have a certain amount of talent, yet beyond that, a good portion of the parts can go to students who fit in the costume or who are the correct height to form a unified group on stage. Students can receive the same part as last year because they still fit in the costume and will take less time to rehearse, since they already know the choreography.

All members of a certain dance ensemble may need to be the same height; they may have to match a partner or even resemble a dancer in the company they will be working with. Some directors want the leads to have a certain hair color. Directors look at many factors when bringing students into a professional production.

Skills that are always appreciated include the student's ability to pick up steps and apply corrections quickly, respect for the rehearsal process, ability to wait your turn without playing around in the studio, and physical presentation. In a ballet audition, for example, girls should put their hair up in a neat bun, and boys should make sure their hair is out of their face. Appropriate ballet clothing includes a leotard and pink tights for girls and tights and tucked-in T-shirts for boys. Proper presentation shows you are serious about what you are doing.

It can be a sad fact that in the world of nonprofits and foundation-supported schools and companies, a substantial donor's child may receive special treatment or casting. It is very rare, though, that a child will get a lead role without the talent needed to execute it. The studio or company is presenting themselves through these performances and does not want to damage its reputation by putting inferior talent front and center on stage.

Your job as a parent is to support and console your child if necessary. It does no good to speak badly about other students who you deem unworthy of a part. Focus on encouraging your student to continue working hard and help them understand that not all the factors are within their control.

—⚬—

In a TV show about dancers, the lead characters auditioned for a Broadway show. Hundreds of dancers showed up at the audition. They all lined up, and the choreographer went down the rows saying yes or no to each person without seeing one step of dance. Then once he weeded out the look he didn't want, he started giving the dance steps so he could choose those with the skills he was looking for.

—⚬—

Students in audition for a summer dance program
Photo by Michael Cook, courtesy of
Tempe Dance, Tempe, Arizona

Taking an Audition

When going to an audition, be prepared for anything. Bring all the shoes necessary for the types of dance your student can do. Women should bring all types of hair fasteners for different styles. Arrive with plenty of time to warm up and sign in.

Read and follow the instructions given for the audition. If they ask for pink tights and black leotards, give them that. Most companies or choreographers don't want to take a chance on people who are not dependable and attentive.

—⚬—

Katie Langan, chair of dance at Marymount Manhattan College, feels that if a student doesn't show up for an audition in the requested dress code "...that's indicative of what my future may be like with that student." Failing to follow directions is a red flag.
Dance Magazine, *February 2014*

—⚬—

The adjudicators will notice how students behave between combinations. Are dancers listening to the corrections of others? How do they treat the other dancers? Are they considerate or ruthless? It takes balance to show you want to be chosen without presenting as too pushy or a troublemaker.

Tell your student not to limit his or her options by showing up dressed or with hair set for a certain part; that may limit the possibility of being considered for other parts.

Simplicity is the best bet, with minimal jewelry and no skirts or leg warmers. Do some research; some adjudicators are notable for being drawn to a certain type or color. One famous teacher is known to give preference to students who wear white. Students who are auditioning for a backup dancer or a show should check out what the dancers who are already working wear and how they present themselves.

School Performances

Most schools have an end-of-the-year performance or recital. It is not uncommon for the school to send out permission forms or agreements for parents to sign. Read these forms carefully; they usually include fees, rehearsal expectations, and performance commitments. Do not be surprised if you cannot pick and choose which rehearsals or performance dates you want your student to attend. Forms could contain a clause about exclusion from performance if rehearsals are missed. A performance takes an enormous amount of preparation from directors and faculty. They must find music, pick out and order or sew costumes, and secure a venue for the show.

Schools may schedule all the rehearsals within the class time; others will have extra evening and weekend rehearsals. Recreational programs may be more lenient as to their expectations than a school focused on giving students the skills necessary for possible professional careers. Either way, it is essential that your student attend the classes and any extra rehearsals. Entrances and exits must be worked out, as well as spacing. This can best be done when all the cast is available.

It doesn't really matter if your student can do the entire dance for you in the living room or backyard. Students must be able to perform the dance to the music, in time with the other students. They need to know their spacing and learn to deal with mistakes possibly made by other students or themselves.

—⟋⟍—

In a delightful scene in the animated movie Despicable Me, *the evil (yet soon-to-be-enlightened) character, Gru, wants his adopted daughters to help him in his dastardly deeds. The girls, Margo, Edith, and Agnes, come out of the house dressed for dance, explaining they are expected at rehearsal. No amount of cajoling from Gru will persuade them to miss their dance recital rehearsal. I laughed out loud while watching it. I have seen many times that students, being part of the development of the performance, understand the importance of the*

> *rehearsal process more clearly than their parents do.*

—∿—

It is not overstepping bounds for a school to expect your child to miss birthday parties or other extracurricular activities to attend rehearsals or class.

If a class contains twenty kids and each child misses only one rehearsal, the teacher or choreographer might never have a full cast to rehearse before putting them on stage.

Equally important are the staging rehearsals at the theater where the show will be performed. A school will rent a facility for the show and have only a few rehearsals to space the students and run the dances on the stage where they will be performing. Unless a child is very ill, they need to be at these rehearsals. Not only could they end up completely lost on stage, but also they could ruin the performance for their peers who have been at the spacing rehearsals.

Costumes

Different studios will have varying policies on costuming for their annual, company, and competition performances.

Dance students may be responsible for paying for the costumes they will need for the show. In this case, they will own the costumes afterward. Other studios, and studio companies, retain their costumes and reuse them for future performances. Dancers may still be required to pay a

Seamstress at work in a costume shop
Photo by Lynn Battenberg, courtesy of Scottsdale
School of Ballet, Scottsdale, Arizona

costuming fee to cover cleaning, storage, and fitting of the costumes. New costumes are occasionally added to the collection through this funding, as well as through company budgeting and donations.

Whether you own the costume or are borrowing it, you should follow certain rules to keep the costume in the best possible condition.

—⚜—

In a professional setting the cost of a costume can run into the thousands of dollars. In community theater the budget may not be as high, as these productions often rely on volunteers to help sew the costumes. These people put a lot of time and effort into their work, and the company hopes costumes will withstand the test of time. Their work deserves and must be afforded the same respect and care as the more expensive variety. This is why the care of costumes is an important part of dance education. Some studios do not teach proper care of costumes. Students in these studios wear their costumes to the theater and are allowed to eat and drink in them with no regard for the possibility of ruining the costume. Should they ever find themselves in a professional setting in dance or theater, their ignorance of proper costume care could cause them embarrassment or earn them a reprimand.

—ɯ—

As much as possible, keep costumes free of wrinkles and stains. This is usually done by keeping them in the dressing rooms at the theater or by covering them with a garment bag and hanging them in the dancer's home before and between performances. Only wear costumes in the studio or theater for dress rehearsals, professional photographs, and performances. Costumes should never be worn for play before they are used in the performance.

Once in costume, dancers should stop eating and drinking anything but water. Even water may stain certain fabrics. It is a good idea to wear a robe over the costume if there will be a long wait before going on stage. Sitting in a costume, depending on the costume, may cause wrinkles, loss of fluff, or a dirty seat in the costume. Obviously, these flaws all detract from the magic of the performance.

Professional Performances

When working with a company or with professional or pre-professional theater groups, you must realize that the performance will come first for the director. Directors will not baby your child, nor will they consider schoolwork, for the most part.

This is not to say the performance will be an unkind or unpleasant experience, but you and your student will be expected to do as asked. Your director may be very organized and have rehearsals planned out in advance, or your director may choose from day to day which dancers need to work the next day, and you will be expected to accommodate those requests.

—⟋⟍—

In more cases than not, the student can go with the flow and enjoy the experience more easily than a parent struggling to organize the family life.

—⟋⟍—

The reward is, of course, the time on stage, the ability to learn from professionals, and the applause of an enthusiastic audience.

VIII

Competitions and
Summer Programs

Competitions

Like dance studios, dance competitions vary greatly in their offerings. Some are structured to benefit the artistry and performance of the students; others are designed mostly for fun and the monetary benefit of the owners of the competition.

For classical ballet, there are a few notable competitions. One of the most prominent is the Youth American Grand Prix (YAGP), under the artistic direction of founder Larissa Saveliev. This group holds a variety of regional competitions throughout the United States and in other countries, including Mexico, Brazil, France, Italy, and Japan. A student may qualify to move on to the final competition or to attend the classes offered during the final competition in New York City. Summer scholarships, year-round scholarships, and professional contracts are among the prizes available to the contestants.

The gold, silver, and bronze medal winners also receive financial prizes. Each year, over thirty of the world's leading dance academies and dance companies send representatives to the YAGP New York City finals. These schools and companies submit scholarships or job offers through the YAGP, which then extends them to the students. Dance and ballet competitions are held throughout the year in locations around the world. How involved your dance studio chooses to get and which competitions, if any, it selects depend on the studio's philosophy and focus.

—⁓—

Competitions in the art of ballet have brought out a variety of perspectives. Some lament the focus on physical tricks and the associated loss of concentration on core technique and artistry. Others think competitions provide the best opportunities to show off students to potential scholarship opportunities or jobs.

—⁓—

National competitions for jazz, lyrical, and tap dance tour the United States weekly. Some competitions offer a juried panel and award trophies and small cash prizes to individuals and group dances. These prizes rarely equal the combined cost of the performance and costuming fees. Other groups offer a weekend of master classes along with an evening of competitive performances. Working professionals as well as retired performers or teaching professionals, may teach these classes.

—m—

A parent of a successful Irish step dancer who was participating in the world-championship competition lamented in the movie Jig that, "If I had known what it entailed, I don't know if we would have started this." With the costs of lessons, costumes, and travel for the whole family, the time and financial commitments were enormous.

—m—

One dance competition company, New York City Dance Alliance, awards exceptional prizes to qualified student participants. They have reached out to notable schools and universities to award scholarships to students who compete at the highest level. Producers and choreographers from Broadway shows, as well as touring groups, attend the competition finals with an eye out for possible candidates for their productions. A four-year scholarship to a college or a job in the business is worth the cost of participation. According to the alliance's website, since 2010, they have awarded close to $5,000,000 in college scholarships in conjunction with their college partners. Their goal is to offer scholarships ranging from $2,500 to $5,000 from their own foundation toward the recipient's college of choice.

—⚹—

The owner of a competition studio, who walked away with a dispro-portionate number of scholarships for his students, was asked for his secret. The answer he gave: "A strong ballet program." Although not the main focus of the studio, the classes were taught by qualified classical ballet teachers and taken seriously by the students adding to their technique in other dance forms

—⚹—

All these competitions offer an opportunity to perform on stage, and since dance *is* a performing art form, many studio owners, parents, and students consider that oppor-tunity worthwhile. The preparation and time on stage are valuable even for the recreational dancer. As with all choices, competition costs need to be taken into consider-ation. Parents should not be pushed into a circumstance they cannot afford.

—⚹—

Of two boys who began their train-ing with me, one stayed with the company-associated school and the other went to train with a school focused on ballet competitions. At the age of seventeen, both boys were sought out for opportunities with one of the top ballet companies in New York City. One received his offer through a competition; the other received his after taking an audition class. A competition is a great way to garner opportunities, but families who cannot afford the costs can find other ways to succeed. Although these two students took different tracks, both were rewarded for their hard work. Success ultimately comes from your student's skills.

—⟋⟍—

Conventions/Conferences

Conventions often have a competition component, but they also offer classes to students and, occasionally, teachers.

Working professionals, retired dancers, or renowned teachers often lead the student classes. However, a friend of the director may also teach classes. So, do your homework and find out who will be teaching your child.

—⁂—

Gus Giordano taught a master class at a local competition studio. He had his own style (as well as a dance company bearing his name) and extensive knowledge about proper warm-ups and the sequence of a jazz class. He was giving away pearls of wisdom as he spoke to the students. The next day the students and, sadly, the jazz teacher from the studio complained that the class had been too slow; they had spent too much time warming up and working on isolation and technique. They wanted to be moving and jumping. How sad that they missed the gifts this teacher shared with them.

—⁂—

Convention classes are similar to master classes in that they are usually huge. Often they take place in convention centers with carpeted rooms. The teacher, who usually stands on a raised platform, may have assistants who help them show the steps or routines presented.

Due to the class size, students receive little individual correction or direction. Instead, students derive benefit from these classes by receiving knowledge from professionals and getting out of the familiar and secure environment of a home dance studio.

—〰—

I observed a convention class where the teacher, in a sincere effort to teach the students a routine, taught the entire class with her back to the students. She was giving directions and encouragement but had no idea whether the students were picking up the steps or not. Students may have found benefit from the challenge of the routine, but not from a true teaching situation.

At another convention, the teacher came down from the stage, leaving his assistants to lead the combinations, and walked through the students while handing out as many personal corrections as he could.

—〰—

Summer Programs

Summer dance programs can offer a fun way to continue dance study. Some programs are for dancers bound for a professional career, but plenty provide good training with a minimum of competitive push. Both *Pointe* and *Dance Magazine* dedicate part of their January issues to summer dance programs. They contain many full-page advertisements, as well as a list of programs that is less eye catching but reasonably complete.

Before committing to a program, parents need to assess the maturity and readiness of their student to attend. Attending a summer program alone can be a challenge for your students younger than fifteen. If you feel your student needs a program outside of your town, consider going with them. Either offer to chaperone the program, or find housing for the summer in the town where the program is being held and have your child attend as a day student, not a boarder.

Home studios or other studios or community centers in your city may offer their own summer programs. Some programs bring in guest teachers to augment or replace their staff for summer. These programs can provide a great way for students to experience a variety of teaching styles without having to leave home. It also allows students to see how they stack up in a class of dancers outside the comfort of their own studio.

If your student is ready for a boarding summer program, do your research to find out what the program offers in way of room and board. A program may offer a fully supervised dorm situation that provides meals as part of the package. Others may have dorms or apartments that offer no supervision or meal plans. These students are left to their own devices to get to class, go to bed at a reasonable hour, and find proper nutrition. Your student's maturity will dictate how much support he or she will need to have a successful summer experience.

—⁓—

If your student wants to dance as a profession, an offer of a summer scholarship shows that the studio or company is willing to invest in your student. This is an advantage and honor for your student, but he or she must look at the company offering the scholarship as well, to ensure that the style and repertoire fit with the student's needs.

—⁓—

Like with standard study, you need to choose summer programs carefully. There are many types of programs in locations around the world. Their costs differ as much as their locations; many offer the possibility of scholarships. Techniques vary from ballet, modern, hip-hop, jazz, and musical theater; the Rockettes even have their own summer camps, where they occasionally pick up dancers for their shows. To get the most for your money, scout for the professionalism and quality of teaching of different programs. Online dance-parent chat groups can give you an idea of what other parents think of the program. Other parents can tell you the experiences their students had there; read carefully and ask questions.

—∞—

I looked on one dance-parent chat group and found a mother going on and on about a great summer program her son had attended. After further discussion, it seemed her fondness for the program hinged totally on the fact that her son was able to acquire a job from one of the visiting teachers, not necessarily on the fact that the training was of benefit to his skills.

—∞—

Good teaching does not only happen at the top ballet company studios or places with Broadway in the title. Both, School of American Ballet, school of New York City Ballet and the Jacqueline Kennedy Onassis (JKO) School, school for American Ballet Theater, located in New York City, have excellent programs, but they may not be what your student needs right now. Kee Juan Han, the director of the Washington School of Ballet who wrote a foreword to this book, is well known for his teaching skills and summer program. The Pacific Northwest Ballet, in Seattle, Washington, are among many who offer a strong summer program worth looking into.

Perhaps your student would enjoy a summer working with the Rockettes, even though he or she has no desire to become one as a profession. Experimenting with different dance forms open possibilities and minds, and summers are a great time to do that.

—ᴡᴡ—

While still in junior high school, having only had ballet training, I attended a summer program in my hometown that focused on musical theater. It was so much fun. I was able to dance in a different manner and meet actors and musicians who were as in love with performing as I was. It opened up my perception of performing.

—ᴡᴡ—

Earl Mosley's Institute of the Arts offers a summer intensive program. Mr. Mosley, an alumnus of Alvin Ailey Dance Theater, has taught at that school, other schools, and universities. *Dance Teacher* magazine named him Dance Teacher of the Year in 2005. His summer program offers a variety of scholarships and is particularly focused on a diverse student population. The program offers modern dance, ballet, jazz, hip-hop, African dance, composition, and repertory. The students perform at the end of each week, and all participants of the program, from beginner to advanced, are cast in at least one piece of choreography. For the month of July, the program rents out a private school in the small, bucolic Connecticut town of Kent.

Earl Mosley teaches in an outside studio
during his summer program.
Photo by Steffen Coleman, courtesy of Earl Mosley's Institute
of the Arts, Dance on the Mountain Summer Program.

Earl Mosley's Institute of the Arts is an example of a wonderful summer experience that does not advertise in the dance magazines, as it uses all its funds toward its scholarship program. Yet, it is a reputable program that gives most of its accepted students at least a partial scholarship. This summer program is attended by students from all over the United States and several different countries. When you're searching for summer programs, the Internet and word of mouth can be your friends.

Jacob's Pillow in Lee, Massachusetts, has been offering summer programs since the 1940s. Presently it offers

The "barn" studio at Jacob's Pillow summer dance program. Above, Didy Veldman rehearses with contemporary program participants in preparation for their Inside/Out performance. Photo by Kristi Pitsch

specialty sessions including ballet, modern/contemporary, jazz, hip-hop, and musical theater. The students study these dance forms in two or three week programs and perform at the end of that time. World-famous teachers and choreographers come to teach and set pieces for the students. The current program has a highly competitive audition process and has a scholarship component.

The program takes place on the campus of Jacob's Pillow, in the Berkshire Mountains. The students stay in cabins and take class in rustic studios. The Pillow also houses two theaters that run a full summer program, which students are able to attend, for performing artists from throughout the world.

Summer programs are a great time to explore different dance styles, teachers, and contemporaries to see how students compare and what they need to work on. These programs can also help students develop lasting friendships, as well as an understanding of the artistic component of the dance world.

IX

Parenting a Dancer

Preparing for class
Photo by Lynn Battenberg, courtesy of Bender Performing Arts,
Phoenix, Arizona

One of the best things you can do for a child who is deeply involved in dance is to stay levelheaded. By creating a grounded home life, you are supplying a solid support system and a constant and dependable environment. Even when everything is going well, the serious pursuit of dance can be physically exhausting and emotionally draining. Coming home to a nurturing environment will be a welcome respite. Dinners and family discussions, beyond the topic of dance, will help keep your child's feet firmly on the ground. This does not mean that you should ignore the accomplishments or disappointments your child may experience in dance; it means that those experiences should not hold the full focus of the entire family.

At some point, classes and rehearsals may dominate your child's life, but when he or she is not expected in class or rehearsals, going to the movies or to a concert that has nothing to do with dance can add to your child's development as a happy, healthy human being. Allow your child the opportunity to experience life outside of dance.

Parental Etiquette in the Studio

Just as there are socially accepted behaviors in a restaurant, there are also appropriate behaviors for parents in a dance studio. Some people feel that because they paid for their meal, they should be able to behave any way they wish. Some parents of dance students feel that because they are paying for classes, they may behave as they please. In neither case does the poor behavior turn out well for offenders or for people with whom they are associated

Do your homework before choosing a studio so that you have an appropriate level of respect and confidence in the program and its' staff. Then, let the staff do their job. Be aware that the studio is attempting to teach all students to the best of their ability. This does not always translate into teaching everyone in the same way, because each student has a different combination of gifts and needs.

As previously stated, parents have the right to seek knowledge about their child by asking questions, as opposed to demanding or making personal attacks on the studio staff.

The choreographer decides the casting. Parents do not have a voice in these decisions. It is not unusual for schools to give graduating dancers special parts, regardless of their level of talent, as a reward for being with the studio for years.

This is not always the case. If your child is not as talented, or is not deemed right for a particular part, then he or she may be passed over for another dancer, whom you, as a parent, may not consider as deserving as your child. Watching your disappointed child may be difficult, but it is not appropriate for you to make demands. Instead, think of this as an opportunity to sympathize with your child, comfort his or her hurt feelings, encourage hard work and perseverance, and compliment his or her progress.

Criticizing the dancer who got the part, or the choreographer who made the decision, may cause a rift between people who have to work together. It also shows a lack of respect for other people's perspective, experience, and expertise, and it encourages excuses and blame rather than self-examination and determination.

Fortunately, or perhaps unfortunately, parents do not always recognize the flaw in their child's performance that a teacher or choreographer may see.

The specific skills for the dance, and the proper dancer for his or her vision is recognized by the choreographer or director alone, not the parents. A gifted dancer will end up on top. All types of studios want to show off the talented students they have painstakingly developed. So, while a lesser talent may take the place of your student in the back row, stage right, they most likely will not take your gifted child's role as the lead.

—◊—

"There is only one pretty child in the world, and every mother has it."
Chinese proverb

—◊—

The Hardworking Child

Passion and hard work are essential to success in dance, but they are not always enough to create a professional. A person can give it their all, show up to every class and rehearsal, and still realize that another student is more talented. This is part of the heartbreak of any art form.

—◊—

One of the focuses of the film Amadeus is the rivalry between composers Mozart and Salieri. In one scene, Salieri wonders why God was so cruel as to give him a strong desire to compose music without giving him the talent required to succeed. Sadly, this is a curse many dancers also face.

—〰—

Supportive and well-meaning parents see the hard work and desire their children have for dance. They also see the beauty their child creates. They may miss the flaws a teacher or choreographer sees that keep that child from earning solo roles. These flaws may include feet that are not stretched fully, or are slightly sickled, lack of stage presence or emotion, lack of strength and endurance, unflattering lines, or an inability or unwillingness to take correction and make improvements.

Some parents are under the impression that when the star of the studio moves on, whether to another studio, to college, or to a professional career, it means everyone moves up the ladder.

That is only partly correct. Your child does not magically improve to star quality as a result of the exit of another student. Your child's skill level may not be affected by others at the studio. On the other hand, taking classes with other hardworking and focused students may improve your child's focus, and that may or may not translate into better technique.

Your child may be in a position for consideration for more or different roles, but there are no guarantees. If your child is of an equal or higher level of talent than the exiting student, he or she may step into plum parts after the other student departs. If the school does not deem your child as being at the same level as the departing student, they may alter the parts for his or her level of accomplishment, or they may not open the opportunities to your child at all.

Some studios reward their departing seniors with a special role in their last performance; although not necessarily the leading part. Studios do not usually give out parts in a show; particularly lead parts, based on loyalty to the studio or seniority. They award these parts based on ability and talent.

—∿—

A graduating student was given a part in a trio. Her mother felt having been at the studio for 14 years that her student should have had a solo part, and spoke to the director of the school. What the mother was unaware of was that her daughter's dedication and focus for dance, through high-school, had waned and she had not improved in technique or strength. Just showing up to classes until graduation is not enough to be featured in a performance.

—⚬—

Here again, it is your job as a parent to console your child's disappointments and to encourage that child to do his or her best with the role he or she has received. Help your child to emotionally deal with the disappointment so it does not stand in the way of his or her enjoyment of dancing.

The Studio Star

You may be lucky enough to have the star student in your family. Your child may be the one who gets attention from teachers and great parts from choreographers. Of course, your family's values will help dictate how you and your child behave in these circumstances. You may enjoy bragging rights and encourage your child to do the same.

Keep in mind several things, including that your child may be at the top in your local studio but may not be the top of his or her profession should he or she choose a career in dance. Should your child go on to pursue a dancing career, he or she will have to deal with directors and choreographers of stature who, for the most part, do not enjoy working with dancers who behave as if they are superior to others in the performance.

You can help your child balance success with humility. Do you really want your child to be the best but have no friends or support system outside the home? Eventually children move away from home and have to live in a world of people who do not love them as their mother and father do. If you want to raise a successful dancer, help your child enjoy dance not only when achieving the top spots; help your child appreciate the process of working with other dancers to achieve a successful performance.

A Word for Fathers of Male Students

Advanced male dancers at the Washington School of Ballet
Photo by Media4Artist, Theo Kossenas. Photographs provided
courtesy of Washington Ballet and the Washington School of Ballet

At this writing, a boy in dance, to the uneducated, still holds a stigma of not being "manly" enough, despite the fact that it takes strength and talent equal to, if not greater than, that of any athlete in any sport. A father's bond to his son is special and important to a young man's development into an emotionally healthy adult. Standing behind your son who has found an interest in dance is a gift. If he has the talent to back up the desire, you are luckier still. Like with sports, one does not have to be the team star to benefit from the experience.

In the United States, many male dance students do not talk about their studies outside the dance studio, and they often hide the fact that they dance from their friends. Whereas girls may be envied for their grace and coordination, boys feel the judgment of age-old prejudice.

—⁂—

A family with a daughter in ballet lessons found their son was interested in taking classes. Initially, he liked his summer ballet program, but at eight years old, he did not enjoy being the only boy in the class. He left ballet and enrolled in martial arts classes. After a few lessons in aikido, he got into a fight at school and flipped a kid onto his back. Fighting was not acceptable in the household or the school. The boy was sent back to ballet class, where he learned self-control, respect, and other things, except the combat taught in martial arts. Once their son was back in ballet, the parents found that it helped tremendously with his attention deficits, and his schoolwork improved. At the age of fifteen, he now sees being one of the few boys in class differently than he did at age eight.

—⚬—

Gay Men in Dance

Dance has a reputation for having a large number of gay men. The percentage of gay men in dance is greater than in the general public, as is the number of gay men in every art form. This could be because there is comparatively little prejudice toward homosexuals in the arts. Dancers are judged by their talents and artistic contributions, not by their sexual orientation. This creates a welcoming atmosphere not always found in the "outside world."

Dance is also a boon for straight men because it is filled with beautiful women. More than a few male dancers entered the field of dance so they could mingle with the lovely ladies.

—⚬—

"Mom, it's like Christmas every day," a male student told his mother about being a straight male dancer at an arts school.

—⚬—

Children's sexuality is set at birth. If they enjoy dancing, support them in their studies. Dance will not change who they are, but it may allow them to gain the self-confidence they need to develop into the people they are meant to be, whether gay or straight.

—⧈—

Your son can no more "catch" homosexuality from a gay man than he can "catch" intelligence from a Mensa member.

—⧈—

Bullying

The issue of bullying has gained attention in public and private schools, as well as in dance schools. This behavior, once brushed off, as "kids will be kids," is no longer ignored. The true and lasting effects of bullying, both physical and emotional, have become glaringly apparent.

Boys seem to take the brunt of harassment outside of the studio, while girls are more apt to experience it within a studio setting. How bullying affects your child depends as much on his or her personality as it does on parenting.

—⧈—

One of my students, now a professional, told me he was not bullied at all. Upon further discussion, it came out that he had, in fact, been verbally harassed, but he only considered physical abuse to be bullying. He felt that since he could easily let the taunts roll off his back, they did not matter.

—⟋⟍—

Sometimes children will not bring the problem to their parents because they worry that any parental intervention will make matters worse. If bullying becomes a serious problem, children may give other, less straightforward clues. They may look and act sad or experience outbursts of anger. As these are also signs of adolescence, it can be hard for a parent to know the difference. Students may be more prone to confide in a friend.

—⟋⟍—

Other parents at the dance studio were the first to alert the parents of a male dancer that he was having difficulties with bullies at school. He had confided in their children, who then told their parents. The parents, in turn, concerned for the boy's welfare, alerted his parents. Because he enjoyed dancing, he did not want to worry his parents or risk being taken out of classes.

—⟋⟍—

It is your responsibility to keep your children emotionally and physically safe. Doing so may require extra effort for you and your family if your student truly wants to pursue dance but is being bullied or relentlessly teased at school. Frequently, communities have many educational options that you will probably be able to access a safe environment.

Most public schools have a zero-tolerance policy against bullying; however, the size of a school may make enforcement difficult. Private schools can offer an alternative for those with the funds to pursue them. Charter schools have taken off across the country, and many restrict the size of the classes and have strict and enforceable rules and codes of conduct. There may be an arts school in your community that caters to students pursuing training in the performing arts.

If these opportunities are not available where you live, homeschooling or online schooling may be viable options to keep your student safe.

Quitting

Imagine that your young child has put in a year or two at the dance studio and is not interested in continuing. Now what? It is important that you listen to what your child is saying to you. Know his or her patterns of behavior, parental manipulation, and truthfulness. Regret that you never had the opportunity as a child, or because you wish you had continued studying, is not a valid reason to pressure your child to remain in dance. A child who is not interested in studying dance will not be happy in class and will distract other dance students.

—⟋⟍—

Forcing a child to take dance classes can be likened to the adage about leading a horse to water. You can make your child attend classes, but you cannot make that child work hard or improve any more than you can make the horse drink the water.

—⁂—

Children who do not enjoy dance should not continue. For students younger than eight years old, there is plenty of time to come back to dance with professional aspirations, without a significant interruption in their potential success, assuming that the lapse does not last more than a year or two and that when they return they are ready to work hard. It is never too late to come back to simply enjoy dance.

It is difficult for a parent who has invested many years and much money to have a student who suddenly wants to stop dancing. While parents are open to having their children stop studying dance at the end of high school, they find it difficult to understand children who stops just when they seem to hit their stride.

—⁂—

I have seen instances in which a student wanted to quit or to change studios because of the arrival of a talented dancer who made it necessary to share or lose a starring role. This is

> *another tough choice with which you*
> *can help your child. It is part of the*
> *dance world. Do you want to encour-*
> *age your child to deal with the situ-*
> *ation, see it as a clue that he or she*
> *may not be able to handle dance as a*
> *profession, or decide to find a studio*
> *where she or he can continue to be*
> *the queen or king bee?*

—ϡ—

In these cases, compromise is often the best answer. If your child wants to quit midyear, make an agreement to finish out the year and see if he or she feels the same at the end of the year. A successful performance in the recital may reenergize an ambivalent student. This approach also teaches the value of commitment and team effort. If your child decides to stop dancing at the end of the year, after the performance, suggest taking the summer off and revisiting the choice at the beginning of the school year. Absence may make the heart grow fonder.

If your student is truly set on discontinuing dance studies, take a deep breath and respect that decision. If you fear your child will fall into sloth, you can broker a deal that once out of the studio, your child needs to choose an activity to take its place. If your child worked at the dance studio six days a week, do not expect that level of dedication to a new endeavor right off the bat. Your child may choose a couple of new areas to explore. This is a natural part of discovery of the self and of life goals.

Dance study may take time, patience, and money, but it pays dividends later, when your child is a happy, well-rounded adult with wonderful childhood memories of dance and supportive parents.

—⟋∿⟍—

A longtime and very talented ballet student decided that the life of a dancer was not for her. Still loving the stage, she successfully transitioned to musical theater.

—⟋∿⟍—

X

Educational Choices
and the College Path

Students studying dance should not consider education a backup plan in case a performance career does not work out. Having a broad awareness of the world, literature, history, and other subjects allows a deeper understanding and empathy when performing stories or expressing emotions.

All students in this country benefit from a high-school degree. For most people, college-level learning is just as important. Reluctant college students often point to the few millionaires or movie stars who succeeded without an education—"few" being the operative word.

The performing part of a dancer's career is brief. Having a job and a chance in the dance business is just that—a chance. You can make the best of it, succumb to the harsh reality of the business, suffer a career-ending injury, experience a change of heart, or change career goals for any number of other reasons.

Careers in dance can span anywhere from a couple of years to several decades. The average length of a performing dancer's career is about seven years. A variety of full-time careers associated with dance may arise after a performance career has ended, but these careers are not abundant and are highly sought after.

Professional dancers are the lucky ones—lucky to have been chosen for the job out of the tens of thousands of dance students across the country (and around the world). By conventional wisdom, only about 1 or 2 percent of these students actually dance professionally. With that in mind, a solid academic education is essential.

Homeschooling

Teachers or directors may tell you how talented your child is and how, with more time, they could do so much more for that child. They may do everything but guarantee a successful career in dance, if only you will pull the child out of school to allow for more studio time. You could homeschool them or have them finish high school online.

No one except the director of a company or production can guarantee your child a job. Even then, the director must have a written contract available when your student is ready for the job. And remember, contracts are for a specific period of time and do not renew automatically. Each year, a new crop of students audition for a relatively few positions as professional dancers.

Homeschooling is a huge responsibility for parents. If you are planning to homeschool your child, by all means continue that plan, but do not take it lightly or enter into it without considerable planning, discussion, and preparation.

Other Options

Options besides homeschooling are available for dance students whose school and dance class schedules conflict. For those who can afford it, private schools may accommodate a heavy study and performance schedule. Charter schools, a free option, are available throughout the country. Many cities have either satellite or charter schools that specifically design their academic schedules to allow study of the performing arts.

—⁓—

When choosing a high school, check the school's accreditation. An academically gifted theater student who attended a charter school for the performing arts found upon graduation that she was not eligible for college scholarships because the high school had neglected to obtain the proper accreditation. This lack of accreditation also restricted the colleges or universities to which she could apply.

—⁓—

In a school setting, even at an arts school, all teachers, including math, English, and history teachers, expect their students, even budding artists, to master the skills required by the course. The students may have stars in their eyes, but the teachers keep their feet on the ground.

—✺—

I met one of the original kids cast as Billy in the Broadway show Billy Elliot. *During his experience as Billy, he and the other children in the cast were schooled together while rehearsing and performing the musical. He was able to travel, performing in a variety of countries. When I met him, he was a young man, too tall to play the role of Billy anymore. Understanding the business as he and his parents did, he was back in his local high school to finish his education while taking dance and voice lessons.*

—✺—

For the dedicated high-school student of ballet who does not have access to advanced study in his or her city or town, the United States contains a few boarding schools that combine ballet instruction and high-school education. A student goes through an audition process for acceptance into the program. Some of these programs offer scholarships or help with tuition. These programs have a proven record and the oversight and supervision of a boarding school.

—✺—

A very talented dancer from a tiny midwestern town was sent alone to one of the state's larger cities to study in a reputable studio. This particular studio did not have the structure to accommodate out-of-town students. The student lived with a different family almost every year and changed schools several times. Navigating her dance studies, adolescence, and school, virtually alone, made for a difficult road and added emotional stress to an already emotion-filled environment.

—〰—

College Opportunities

New York University, Tisch School of the Arts
Photo courtesy of Benjamin Kammerle

Dance careers and college education are emphatically not mutually exclusive. There are a variety of ways to follow the path and achieve both.

—⚯—

In an article in the "Lifetime Learns" pullout of Dance Magazine, May 2012, Violette Verdy states:
 [Ballet students] are in the midst of that incredible competition and race—it's technique, it's speed, speed, speed, and they have to be up to par and deliver. They sometimes don't make it. Emotionally, spiritually, they go crazy. They get depressed and overwhelmed. Here at the University, (of Indiana, where she is on faculty) they have time to grow up, to talk about their problems and try to correct them. And if they decide that it's going to be too much for them, they are in the most protective place to make the changes.
 Ms. Verdy was a principal dancer with the New York City Ballet.

—⚯—

If your child receives a paying job or company contract after high school, that is a good indication that he or she has a strong chance in the business. It is not, however, a do-or-die time. Many dancers have successful careers in dance after completing a college degree. A student who may want a bit more training, or who is not emotionally ready to tackle the business world, is better off waiting until he or she can navigate and enjoy a career.

—ᴡᴡ—

I have attended many dance and the-ater performances where the cast biographies boast a majority of the performers with college degrees from reputable dance, ballet, and theater programs throughout the country.

—ᴡᴡ—

University dance programs looking for faculty will recognize the importance of life experience, particularly if the applicant reached the soloist level in a nationally or internationally recognized company, but they prefer or require that most applicants have a college degree.

Students can pursue college at an unhurried but consistent pace to accommodate the fast pace of a dance career. Depending on location, your child may be able to take classes on campus or online. The key to successfully completing a college degree is to choose a school that is properly accredited. That way, most, if not all, classes a student completes may be applied toward a degree regardless of whether the student stays in that school or transfers to another one.

Many modern dancers began their serious training in either liberal arts or fine arts/conservatory college programs, which often offer students a range of experiences with techniques, choreography, and repertory with guest artists.

In many instances, professionals who went to college programs to teach have set choreography on the students or formed companies with the student dancers with whom they enjoyed working. College students might also receive invitations to summer programs.

College programs frequently offer a variety of training experiences and learning opportunities that a dancer would not receive in the professional world. Opportunities to study choreography and to choreograph; to study kinesiology, physiology, and anatomy; and to learn teaching methods to take into the studio are just some of the benefits of a college education.

—⁊⁊⁊—

A fellow dancer in my college ballet program was drawn to modern dance for the first time in her life. She augmented her ballet training with classes and summer programs in modern dance. Upon finishing her degree, she went on to a long and accomplished career with one of the country's top modern dance companies.

—⁊⁊⁊—

Fordham University in New York City opened a satellite campus at Lincoln Center that offers professional dancers academic classes specifically scheduled around company classes, rehearsals, and performances.

When dancers are on hiatus, they may also attend college-level classes, assuming there is a university in the town where they live; otherwise, online classes are available. They may take general education classes at community or two-year colleges, often for less money than they would pay at a four-year university. Again, make sure the college or online degree program is fully accredited to ensure that the credits earned will transfer to a four-year college and that the degree earned is meaningful.

Many high schools offer testing that allow a student to earn credit toward their college degree if the scores are high enough. This can allow a student to enter college as a second-semester freshman or even a sophomore, adding another advantage to finishing a high-school education.

—◊◊◊—

A great resource when looking at higher education is Dance Magazine's *"College Guide."* Pointe *magazine also publishes an annual issue on higher education.*

—◊◊◊—

Author's Notes

—⧗—

"Go into the arts, I'm not kidding. The arts are not a way to make a living. They are a very human way of making life more bearable. Practicing an art, no matter how well or badly is a way to make your soul grow, for heaven's sake. Sing in the shower. Dance to the radio. Tell stories. Write a poem to a friend, even a lousy poem. Do it as well as you possibly can. You will get an enormous reward. You will have created something."

Kurt Vonnegut

—⧗—

Having had dance as a major part of my life, I can say that it has definitely brought me more joy than sorrow.

From the experience of being a student with the hard work and hope of becoming a dancer to the thrill of performance, dance is a gift.

I was lucky that my time studying was filled with friends and fun. Possibly because we were not aware of the realities ahead of us, we blindly threw ourselves into dance. Many of my fellow students are today close and dear friends. We still have the ability to have fun and laugh together. Once we are together, no matter whether we are in public or private, events eventually demand one or more of us to jump up to mimic a dance we once did or a famous dancer we all know.

At a young age I was exposed to a variety of very creative people. It was clear to me early on that kindness and friendship could come in any color, age, or sexual orientation. Prejudice was never an issue; I only cared about what was in the heart.

My skills took me to the studio as a teacher. Although I loved performing, both my skills and the rigors of the lifestyle kept me from a performer's life. Teaching, however, fit like a glove.

I encourage my readers to help your students enjoy the benefits of dance while realizing that performance is not the only way to keep dance in their lives. Supporting dance, teaching, or simply attending performances are all ways of keeping the joy of dance in one's life.

Acknowledgments

So many people helped and supported me in the effort to get this book into print. Thank you to Lynn Trimble, whose idea it was to put my years of educating students and parents into a book. Karen Mendez has supported me for as long as I can remember, in whatever I do, and she knows grammar and spelling. And special thanks to my sister and brother who always have my back.

Many thanks to Jacob's Pillow, the Washington School of Ballet, Earl Mosley's Institute of the Arts, Bender Performing Arts, Tempe Dance, and Scottsdale School of Ballet for sharing photographs.

Thanks to Lynn Battenberg, Michael Cook, Steffen Coleman, Dorcas Guest Nelson, and Chris Lee for their contribution of photographs and support.

These wonderfully encouraging people are all truly appreciated. The following people have helped, encouraged, or contributed toward the completion of this book. You kept me going; thank you.

Dede Albers, Gail Algeo, Erin Arbuckle, Stacy Augustine, Debbie Bain, Kevin and Mari Bender, Linda Biondo, Beth Broeker, Nancy Crowley, Donald and Sibylle Dadey, Dog Eared Bookstore, Miki Casalino, Missy Coyle, John D. Edwards, Donlin and Jenny Forman, Sergey Gordeev, Colleen and Bruce Hallberg, David Hallberg, Kee Juan Han, Sally Hartman, Bob Kammerle, Nadya Kovton, the Lee family, Natalia Magnicaballi, Ken Martinez, Gretta

Miles, Earl Mosley, Betty Johnson Neal, Norton Owen, Susan Paull, Hanna Rubin, Karen Saari, Kim St.Clair, Lydia Sampson, Mimi Solaire, Anthony Spalding, Nancy Stephens, Chelsea Vaughn, Rosie Vergilio, Chelsea Wells, Ann Widmar, Lynn Wise, and Alice Zaney.

About the Author

Graduating from the University of Utah, where she earned both a Bachelor of Fine Arts in ballet and a Master's in education, Betsy Bradley, known to her students as Miss Betsy, has taught ballet for over forty years, most recently with the School of Ballet Arizona. Ms. Bradley began her dance training with Ballet Russe alumni, Roman Jasinski and Moscelyne Larkin. She danced with the Tulsa Ballet Theater and Ballet West's Ballet for Children and has since educated teachers on how to use performing arts to develop children's creativity. She has been featured in newspaper and magazine articles.

Mother of two adult sons, Bradley now lives in Scottsdale, Arizona, where she continues to advocate for the arts and arts education. She has served on the Scottsdale Arts in Education Council board of directors, leading the organization as president for one term. This earned her the Volunteer of the Year award from the Scottsdale Charros, a special activity group dedicated to serving the community.

Ms. Bradley can be reached at:
danceanswers@gmail.com